BASIC SKILLS IN
GCSE English
for AQA A

the date below

Imelda Pilgrim

Consultant: Peter Buckroyd
Experienced examiner

Heinemann

Inspiring generations

Heinemann Educational Publishers
Halley Court, Jordan Hill, Oxford OX2 8EJ
Part of Harcourt Education

Heinemann is the registered trademark of
Harcourt Education Limited

© Imelda Pilgrim, 2003

First published 2003

07 06 05 04 03
10 9 8 7 6 5 4 3 2 1

British Library Cataloguing in Publication Data is available
from the British Library on request.

ISBN 0 435 10603 1

Thanks to Lindsay McNab, Marian Slee, Mike Hamlin and the
English department at Acklam Grange School for their help.

Designed by AMR Ltd
Original illustrations © Harcourt Education Limited, 2003

Illustrations:
pp8, 83, 114 Phil Healey; pp12, 91, 102 Sarah Warburton; pp43, 72, 110, 112 Alice Englander; pp30, 53, 66, 69, 88
Sarah Geeves; pp46, 118, 120 Andrew Quelch; pp35, 39 David Woodroffe

Cover photo © Photodisc
Cover design by Hicksdesign

Printed and bound in Italy by Printer Trento S.r.l.

Photographs:
p9 Car magazine/Tim Wren; p11 Kobal/Newline/Bruce Talaman; p16 Getty; p23 PA News; p24 Alamy; p31 Topham
Picturepoint; p33 Trevor Clifford/Harcourt; Courtesy of Sony Electronics Inc; Corbis; Courtesy of Sony Electronics Inc;
Photodisc; p37 the *Daily Telegraph*; p50 Ricky Tomlinson/BBC; p52 Empics; Rex; Getty; Getty; p54 NHPA; p57
Mirrorpix; p58 Corbis; p64 Mary Evans; p72 Getty; Corbis; Alamy; Alamy; Getty; p87 Bubbles/David Robinson; p93
Corbis; p94 Roger Scruton; p99 Getty; p100 Getty; p105 Robert Harding; p126 Getty; p139 Corbis.

Contents

Section A — Reading

Section B — Writing

Section C — Exam Practice

To prepare for GCSE in English you need to develop your skills in reading and writing. This book takes you through the skills you need to focus on. It will help you build on what you already know and show you how to develop further.

Reading and writing are dealt with separately in this book, to make it easier to follow. They are, however, very closely linked. The work you do on reading will help you with your writing and vice versa. You can choose to work through the sections in the order they appear in the book or to move between 'Reading' and 'Writing'.

As you work through the book you will:
- learn more about the skills you need in the examinations
- do a wide range of activities that will help you develop these skills
- learn how to read questions carefully
- learn how to plan, write and check your answers.

There are also practice papers for you to try, with advice on how to do them, and sample papers for you to do on your own when you are ready.

As you study the texts and work through the activities, you will become more aware of what you are expected to do in the examinations. You will gain in confidence and your skills in English will steadily improve. The effort you make now will help you to prepare for GCSE English and to achieve your best in the examinations.

 This symbol indicates whether a chart can be downloaded from the web. Go to www.heinemann.co.uk/usersupport and click on *Basic Skills in GCSE English for AQA A*. You can then select the chart of your choice.

Just think of how many things you are asked to read or write in a single school day:

Your skills in reading and writing are important in almost every area of your school life. They will continue to be important throughout your life, whether or not you continue with full-time education:

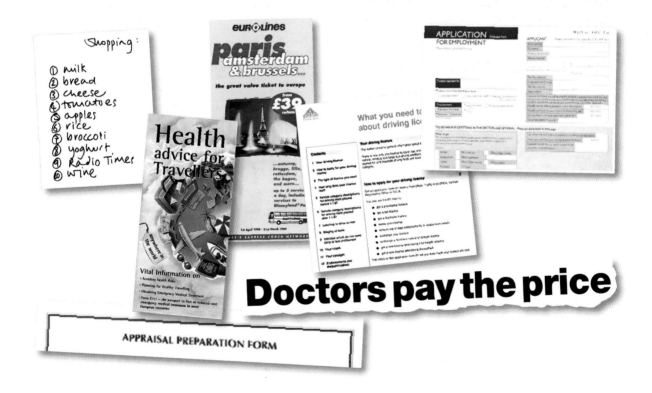

Developing your reading and writing skills

There are things you can do, apart from using this book, to help you improve your reading and writing.

Read as often as you can and as many different things as you can. Make a point of trying to read a newspaper once or twice a week. Look around you and read the leaflets and adverts that you see in public places. Find out more about your favourite sport or interest by reading a magazine about it. If you don't like full-length stories, choose short ones that can be read in half an hour. Pop into your school resource centre and see what's on offer there and start researching subjects on the net.

Think about the things you are reading. Ask yourself: Do they work well? Do they achieve what they set out to do? When you come across new words, use a dictionary to find out what they mean and start to use them in your own writing.

Think about the way you write and the way other people write. Look at the different ways ideas can be organised and sentences put together and start to experiment with these. Set yourself targets: organise your notes with sub-headings if you've never done so before, or try to write two sides for an assignment if you usually write one.

Aim to become more aware of the reading material that surrounds you in your daily life. Think about how you can use what you learn through reading in your own writing. Remember, the progress you make now will stay with you all your life.

Reading Non-Fiction and Media Texts

Non-fiction texts are those that are not made up. They are based on real life, personal experience, facts and/or opinions. They include autobiographies, biographies, journals, diaries, travel writing, leaflets, factual and informative materials.

The media is the general term given to the different forms of mass communication such as television, radio, cinema, the internet, newspapers and magazines. Media texts are those which are found in the media, for example a film, an advertisement or a newspaper article.

In this section you will learn how to:
- read for meaning
- think about presentation
- look at language
- choose the right information
- write about the things you have read.

Reading of non-fiction and media texts is tested in AQA A, GCSE English, Paper 1 Section A.

1 Reading for meaning

Fact and opinion

- A *fact* is something which can be proved to be true, for example:
  The Mini was first introduced in 1959.

- A *false fact* is something which can be proved to be untrue, for example:
  John Ford started the American Ford Motor Company.
  (It was Henry Ford, not John)

- An *opinion* is a point of view which cannot be proved to be true or untrue, for example:
  The Japanese produce the best cars.

Activity 1

1 Copy this chart. Sort the statements below into *facts*, *false facts* and *opinions*. Write the letter of the statement in the correct column. The first one has been done for you:

Facts	False facts	Opinions
		a

   a Car pollution will probably destroy our planet.
   b A car usually has four or five different gears.
   c Most cars have petrol or diesel engines.
   d Formula 1 is a type of car battery.
   e The car is man's best friend.
   f Cars were invented in the seventeenth century.
   g People shouldn't have more than one car.
   h The maximum speed allowed in England is 70 m.p.h.
   i It is difficult to pass your Driving Test.
   j It is illegal to use a mobile phone while driving.

2 Check your answers with a partner. Talk about:
   - how you made your choices
   - how you could check your choices.

Separating fact from opinion

Many things you read are a mixture of *fact* and *opinion*. Read the following newspaper article. It is a mixture of *facts* and *opinions*.

Nightmare fate of a dream machine

By NIGEL BURTON

IT was a Christmas present dreams are made of – a Ferrari F355 Spider resplendent in Italian racing red paintwork, sitting on beautiful alloy wheels.

The driver's wife had bought the hand-made dream machine for £103,000 as the ultimate gift for her car crazy husband.

The thrilled new owner couldn't wait to take it out for a spin.

But a short while later the driver's face was as red as the Ferrari's paintwork – and his car was only fit for a very long stay in the garage bodyshop.

Cleveland Police said the driver lost control along a stretch of road in Thornaby and his dream machine slammed into a metal barrier nose first. The impact spun the car round and shunted its rear into the guard rail. Luckily, the new owner – who had done just 124 miles before the calamitous accident – walked away from the wreck shocked but unscathed.

Police generously declined to name the car's owner last night to spare him from further embarrassment.

'As if it wasn't bad enough smashing up such an expensive car, to wreck the wife's Christmas present must have added insult to injury,' said a force spokesman.

The car was removed by recovery men and taken to a specialist repairer on Tyneside for repairs which could cost as much as £30,000.

Garageman Graham Abel, who recovered the damaged car, said: 'At least he must have plenty of money to get it fixed. It isn't every Christmas you find a Ferrari in your Christmas stocking.'

■ **Classic car: A gleaming Ferrari in Italian racing red**

Northern Echo

To separate the facts from the opinions you need to read very carefully. Sometimes you have to break the sentences down and then re-write the ideas in your own words. You can't just copy them out. Re-read the first paragraph.

IT was a Christmas present dreams are made of – a Ferrari F355 Spider resplendent in Italian racing red paintwork, sitting on beautiful alloy wheels.

The *facts* in it are that:

- it was a Christmas present
- the car was a Ferrari F355 Spider
- the colour of the paintwork was Italian racing red
- it had alloy wheels.

The *opinions* are that:

- it was a Christmas present dreams are made of
- it was resplendent (means that it had a splendid appearance)
- the wheels were beautiful.

Write down four more *facts* **and** four more *opinions* taken from the rest of the article. There may be times when you are not sure whether a phrase is a fact or an opinion. Only write down the ones you are certain of. Start your sentences with:

Four more facts are:

Four more opinions are:

Put a full stop after the last bullet point in each sentence.

Questioning facts

We cannot always check facts but there are times when we need to question them, for example when we read the results of surveys. A *survey* is an examination of a particular issue. It is usually carried out through the use of a questionnaire. People are asked to give answers to different questions. Their answers are then collected together to produce statistics.

As a result of a survey something may appear to be a 'fact', but ...

A. The way the questions are worded makes a difference.

Think about this survey result:

90% favour war

Look at the following two questions. Which of them do you think produced this result? Explain your answer.

1 Which would you prefer:
   a) To go to war   b) To wait until we are attacked?

2 Which would you prefer:
   a) To go to war   b) To work together for peace?

B. The people who complete the questionnaire make a difference.

80% of pocket money goes on sweets

What difference would it make if the children questioned were all under 8?

C. The place where the survey is carried out makes a difference.

Eight out of ten people holiday abroad this year

What difference would it make if the survey was taken outside a travel agent?

Always question how surveys have been carried out before accepting the results as *facts*.

Questioning opinions

A *review* is an assessment of something. You will find reviews of books, CDs, videos, computer games and TV programmes in all newspapers and magazines. In a review the writer expresses his or her *opinion* in order to influence the way the reader thinks.

Activity 3

Read the following review of the DVD of **Blade II**:

The first sentence contains two *opinions*. These are highlighted for you.

1 **Either** copy the whole review and highlight, in different colours, as many opinions as you can **or** as you read, pick out and list at least five more opinions.
2 What does the writer want the reader to think about:
   - the movie
   - the DVD?
   Give a reason for each of your answers.

rent this!

Something of a misfire as a movie, Blade II certainly makes a good DVD. Director Guillermo Del Toro pulls out all the stops. Unfortunately he pulled out too many – here, more is definitely less. The movie is swamped with ideas, some good: ninja vamps, vampires that feed on vampires. Some bad: the hoary old Aliens-style commando gang is dug up again. But the movie seems to have been edited with a liquidiser.

The DVD, however, is great. Two discs, including an informative commentary from Del Toro and an amusing one from Wesley Snipes. Deleted scenes, art gallery, interactive documentaries, music video, director's notes. Three hours of interesting extra material is enough to make you forgive the weaknesses of the movie itself.

Guardian 'Guide'

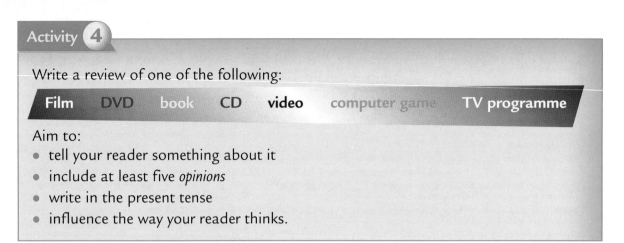

Write a review of one of the following:

| Film | DVD | book | CD | video | computer game | TV programme |

Aim to:
- tell your reader something about it
- include at least five *opinions*
- write in the present tense
- influence the way your reader thinks.

Following an argument

When making a case for or against something, the writer presents the reader with an *argument*. To build an argument the writer uses key points to develop a *point of view*.

To follow an argument you need to be able to:
- identify the key points
- identify the evidence used to support the key points
- ask questions about the text.

Read the following extract and then work through Activities 5, 6 and 7.

Violence, Horror and Popular Entertainment

I don't know what girls need, but it's clear to me that boys need to process horror and violence – because it's so much a part of the world they feel surrounded by.   **1**

When Alexander was still five years old, a neighbour overheard the conversation he was having with her own five-year-old. It concerned the videos they were going to watch that evening. 'Ahhhh,' she cooed, 'they want to watch *Thomas the Tank Engine.*'

'No!' Alexander said quite indignantly, 'we want to watch *Terminator Two* first and then we want to watch *Thomas the Tank Engine.*'

They are two very different sorts of films but they existed equally   **2**
in these little boys' affections. The Arnold Schwarzenegger picture is an outstanding action film. A multi-weaponed cyborg built on a hyper-alloy combat chassis comes back from the future to – oh, never mind. It's a terrific piece of work for those of us who like that sort of thing. The swearing, the fighting, the brutality, the explosions are all first class. You may think it's a little out of the ordinary for a five-year-old. But there we were: Alexander enjoying *Terminator Two* and *Thomas the Tank Engine.*

As he's matured, if that's the right word, this has become even   **3**
more extreme. At the age of ten he likes mutant zombies' heads being blown off just as much as he likes *Teletubbies.* Alexander loves cyber violence, he loves *Beany Babies.* He loves flying body parts, he loves *Winnie the Pooh.*

    4
They're boys, they're sentimental and gruesome. On the walls of his classroom hang examples of history course work. A Tudor time-line shows the kings and queens illustrated with historical details. All the pages that have axes, spears, dripping blood and severed heads are done by boys.

'Do girls produce this sort of revolting violence?' I asked him.

'No,' Alexander snickered. 'The girls just do what the teacher tells them to. The boys try and find some way of making the most of it.'
    5
So my view is that the need to deal with horror and violence is a part of boys, beyond culture. We can worry about what violence is doing to boys but it won't do any good. They're going to turn out their own way.

The Boys Are Back in Town by **Simon Carr**

Identifying key points

The key points are the *main* points the writer makes. They form the skeleton of the *argument*. The key points 1–5 have been numbered in the text for you. Look back and read them again. Talk about what they mean.

Activity 5

You need to explain the writer's argument. Complete the following chart by using your own words to explain the key points. The first one has been done for you.

Key points	What the writer means
1 It's clear to me that boys need to process horror and violence – because it's so much a part of the world they feel surrounded by.	*He says that boys need to deal with horror and violence because it's part of their world.*
2 They are two very different sorts of films but they existed equally in these little boys' affections.	
3 As he's matured, if that's the right word, this has become even more extreme.	
4 They're boys, they're sentimental and gruesome.	
5 So my view is that the need to deal with horror and violence is a part of boys, beyond culture.	

Identifying evidence

Writers often give *evidence* to support their key points. As a reader you need to be able to identify the *evidence* they give.

Match the statements on the left side with the evidence on the right side.
When you have matched them correctly, copy them.

1 The writer supports the point that boys need to process horror and violence by saying that

a when Alexander was ten he liked mutant zombies' heads being blown off just as much as he liked **Teletubbies**.

2 We are told that this doesn't change as boys get older because

b Alex says they just do what the teacher tells them to.

3 He says it's not just his son who is like this as

c when his son Alexander was five he liked to watch **Terminator** and **Thomas the Tank Engine**.

4 The writer suggests that it's not the same with girls because

d all the gruesome pictures about the Tudors in his classroom were done by boys.

Asking questions about the text

When reading, it is important to think carefully about what the writer is saying. Some of the evidence a writer uses might add to the argument but you might not agree with it. There may be things written that do not match your experience or the way you see the world.

1 Re-read the writer's *opinions* on **Terminator Two**:

'The Arnold Schwarzenegger picture is an outstanding action film.'

'It's a terrific piece of work...'

'The swearing, the fighting, the brutality, the explosions are all first class.'

   a If you have seen the film, do you agree?
   b Do you think it sounds like the kind of film that is suitable for a five-year-old to watch? Give at least two reasons for your answer.
2 The writer suggests that girls don't deal with violence and horror in the same way as boys. Do you agree? Give at least two reasons for your answer.

Read the following text closely before answering the questions that follow.

Cigarettes increase threat by 70pc say doctors

Girl smokers 'facing breast cancer risk'

Teenage girls who smoke may dramatically increase their risk of later suffering breast cancer, doctors warn today.

A major study has revealed for the first time that young females taking up the habit may trigger changes in developing breast tissue which could lead to thousands more cases of the potentially fatal disease.

Researchers estimate that girls who smoke cigarettes within five years of starting their periods are 70 per cent more likely to develop the cancer.

The lifetime risk of a woman in Britain suffering breast cancer is one in nine. The risk is much lower for younger women, but smoking could increase the threat, it is claimed. Researchers say that in developed countries it might account for an extra 1,000 pre-menopausal breast cancer cases out of 100,000 teenage smokers.

The latest study was carried out by Dr Pierre Band and colleagues from British Columbia Cancer Agency in Vancouver, Canada.

They compared more than 2,000 women – with and without breast cancer – in terms of their history of smoking and took into account risk factors generally known to be linked to the disease.

Women who started smoking within five years of the onset of menstruation were 70 per cent more likely to develop breast cancer than non-smokers, the study found.

Amanda Sandford, of the anti-smoking group ASH, said: 'If further research confirms smoking in your teens has a special risk attached it's very important. The numbers affected could be staggering.'

Dr Stephen Duffy, of Cancer Research UK, said: 'This study suggests an increased risk of breast cancer for women who smoke in their teens. These could be chance findings since the study is relatively small. The picture remains confusing and we need further research.'

Daily Mail

1 Pick out and list five *facts* from the newspaper article.
2 In your own words list the *key points* made in the article.
3 Give two examples of *evidence* which is used to support the argument that teenage girls who smoke may dramatically increase their risk of later suffering breast cancer.
4 What does Amanda Sandford of ASH say?
5 What does Dr Stephen Duffy say that might make you question the results of the research?

2 Thinking about presentation

Identifying different types of texts

Writing can take many different *forms*, for example:
- letters
- stories
- advertisements
- notes.

Make a list of at least four other forms of writing.

Often we can recognise the form of a text just by looking at it. There are clues in the way it is presented.

 Activity 1

Look at the following five texts. Copy and complete the chart below for **Texts B** to **E**. **Text A** has been done for you:

Text	What the text is	Clues in presentation
A	Notes	Heading, sub-heading, bullet points, not sentences, abbreviations
B		

A

PHYSICAL FEATURES

VOLCANOES:
- ◆ approx. 850 active volcanoes in world
- ◆ caused by movement of rock in earth's surface
- ◆ most found in Ring of Fire around Pacific Ocean
- ◆ can erupt with little warning
- ◆ release red hot ash and lava
- ◆ between eruptions called dormant.

B

C

GO-AHEAD FOR WEMBLEY No 2

A new national sports stadium at Wembley got the go-ahead yesterday after years of delay.

A deal to build the £757 million venue, which will seat 90,000, has been finally agreed seven years after the first bids went in.

The bulldozers will move in at 11a.m. on Monday to demolish Wembley and its famous twin towers. FA chief executive Adam Crozier said: 'There's no doubt that Wembley is an icon - wherever you go in the world, people want to talk about Wembley, and they want to see a new stadium.

'We believe we will have the finest stadium in the world.'

The stadium, which will take four years to build, features a soaring 133-metre-high arch, a sliding roof and temporary athletic track.

German bank West LB is loaning £433 million for the project. The FA is paying £148 million and Sport England another £120 million.

Sun

D

5 Heron Lane, Greenwich, LS1 0TE
15th March, 2002

Dear Sir,

I am a fifteen-year-old boy who is very interested in following a career in the sport and leisure industry. My school offers all its Year 10 pupils the opportunity to do two weeks' work experience in June and I was wondering if it would be possible to gain a placement with your company . . .

E

Chapter 1

It was a cold, dark night in the middle of winter when he first heard the voice. It came creeping into his dreams, waking him gently but turning his blood cold as he realised he was no longer sleeping. Softly, hauntingly, it called to him, forcing him to leave his bed and move hesitantly across the room towards the shimmering frost-cracked window.

How information is presented

Features to do with the appearance and organisation of a text are sometimes called *presentational devices*.

To write well about presentational devices you need to be able to:
* identify them
* say what effect they have.

Look at the poster on the following page which is advertising an animal park.

Activity 2

The *presentational devices* used in the poster are numbered. Complete the chart below by matching the following devices to the numbers:

Write it under the correct number.

a heading	e map	i bold print
b sub-heading	f use of colour	j slogan
c logo	g range of fonts	
d photographs	h timetable	

1	2	3	4	5	6	7	8	9	10
b	a	g	i	h	j	e	f	d	c

Activity 3

Complete the following chart by working out what effect the different *presentational devices* have on the reader. Some of them have been done for you. It may help to work with a partner.

Presentational device	Effect on the reader
heading	It attracts attention – the word 'new' makes it sound different
sub-headings	help to organise
logo	
photographs	Show the different types of animals – make the reader want to see them – particularly the parents and babies
map	
use of colour	
range of fonts	Gives variety – makes it look more interesting – helps to separate out the different bits of information
timetable	
bold print	
slogan	

NEW Animals for 2002
Bears, Baboons & Lions
The Official Top Attraction in the Lake District
2 years in succession
(Cumbria Tourist Board Award for Excellence)

South Lakes Wild Animal Park

The North's leading zoo park is a unique safari on foot with many animals wandering free in natural surroundings. Walk with Kangaroos and Emu in the bush, or watch parrots fly free in the trees. See Lemur Monkeys roaming free in the park and absorb the amazing skills of Gibbons, Macaques and Spider Monkeys high up on their canopy of ropes and branches.

EUROPE'S TOP TIGER CONSERVATION CENTRE IS OPEN ALL YEAR

Every day 10am–5pm Winter 10am–4.30pm
Closed: 25th December
DELICIOUS HOT AND COLD MEALS AND DRINKS ARE AVAILABLE ALL DAY IN OUR CAFÉ

Daily Events
Throughout the year

All day	Hand feed the largest collection of Kangaroo species in the world
2.30 pm	Tiger feeding – Unique in Europe

Easter to end of September

12.00 pm	Meet a snake and cure any fears.
12.30 pm	Ape and Monkey Feeding and Keeper Talk
1.00 pm	Rhino Conservation Talk
1.45 pm	Cat Feeding – See their acrobatic hunting skills
2.00 pm	Lemur feeding – you can help us feed them!
2.30 pm	Tiger feeding – Unique in Europe
3.00 pm	All the other animals are fed
3.30 pm	Giraffe feeding and talk

With a Safari Railway, Gift Shop, Adventure Play Area and many picnic areas. NO DOGS ALLOWED.

78 PAGE FULL COLOUR GUIDE BOOK AVAILABLE

Admission

Adults		£7.00
Child (Age 3–15)		£5.00
O.A.P's		£5.00

November - End February Admission Prices Reduced
Please phone for details   PRICES VALID UNTIL 01/01/03.

HOW TO FIND US

From Junction 36 on M6 follow signs on A590 to Barrow

By Train: Connect direct with First North Western Trains at Dalton and Askam stations. For times from your local station phone 0345 484950.
By Bus: contact Stagecoach 0870 6082608 June to September only

Spectacled Bears unique on mainland UK

We don't just talk about conservation, We Do It!

Information Line: 01229 466086 - Don't Forget, FREE PARKING

Writing about presentational devices

Once you are able to identify the main *presentational devices* and their effects you are ready to write about them. Look at the following task.

Write about the presentational devices used in the South Lakes Wild Animal Park poster and say what is important about them.

To do this you need to describe the different devices and their effects.

Activity

Here is a sample answer for the task. The missing parts of the sentences are listed below the sample answer.

Match the numbers to the letters. Make sure they match correctly by reading each completed sentence aloud. Then copy the passage in full to keep as an example of how to write about *presentational devices*.

> The heading is in a large red font and the word NEW is written in capitals to
> ...1... The sub-headings are also mostly written in red. This helps to ...2...
> Bright colours such as red, yellow and orange, are used in the leaflet to ...3...
> Other information is written in white, black or blue print on a coloured
> background. The leaflet includes photographs of animals, a map and a
> timetable. The photographs of the different animals ...4... The map ...5...
> and the timetable ...6... There is also a logo and slogan on the leaflet. At the
> bottom of the leaflet there is the slogan: 'We don't just talk about
> conservation, We Do It!' This ...7...

a organise the information so that the reader can follow it more easily.
b make the reader want to see them, particularly the parents and babies.
c helps the reader to see exactly when different things are happening.
d make it more attractive and to help separate out different bits of information.
e attract attention and make it sound different.
f gives clear information for the driver on how to get there
g emphasises the importance of conservation and makes the reader think about it.

More about presentation

Here are some other *presentational devices,* which you may come across:

Italics and <u>underlining</u>

These are used when a writer wants to emphasise something.
What points are the writers emphasising in these extracts?

> The giant panda has become a symbol of conservation across the world. This is partly because there are *only a few hundred* giant pandas still surviving in the wild.

> URGENT **STOP PRESS!!**
>
> Every penny counts.
>
> The Royal Mint estimates that there are 7 billion pennies in the UK. Yet at least one third of them are sitting idle in old jam jars, milk bottles and down the backs of sofas.
>
> <u>That means 20 million pounds worth of cash is literally doing nothing!</u>

Charts and diagrams

These are used when a writer wants to show you information in a different way.
What information are you given in the following *diagram*?

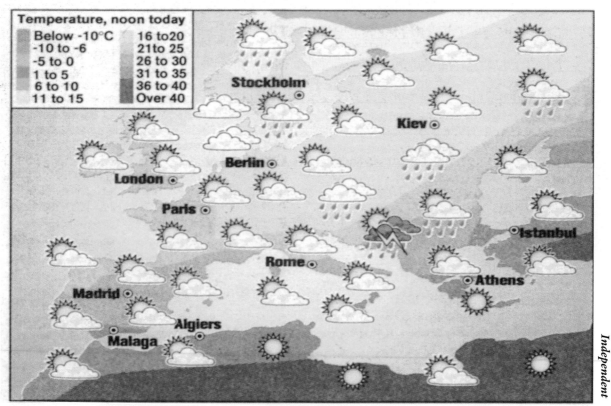

Independent

Give two reasons to explain why the writer chose to present the weather information in this way.

Captions

A *caption* is the short written explanation given with a photograph or illustration. It is the caption which gives the picture its meaning.

Look at this picture. Talk about how the two captions create a different meaning for the same picture.

Crowd watches in horror as Kosgei collapses at tape

Kenya's Kosgei celebrates becoming the first man to crack the hour barrier

In choosing the words for the caption the writer gives the picture meaning for the reader. This technique of fixing the meaning of a picture by the words you place with it is known as *anchoring*.

1 Talk about how you could present the following information in *chart form*:

  a There were twenty-five children in the class. Six of them lived in the town centre and nine were bussed in from the surrounding farms. Of the ten that were left five came from the Kenton Estate and five from the Chophill Estate.

  b **Today's weather in Britain**

    In northern England there is plenty of cloud drifting around with some patches of heavy rain. There will be a light wind with a temperature high of 14°C.

    East Anglia will be bright for a time though showers are expected later. The wind will be light and north-westerly with a temperature high of 14–16°C.

    In the Midlands there will be plenty of cloud though it will stay mainly dry with temperatures reaching 16°C.

    In southern England it will be generally cloudy with sunny intervals especially in the east. The wind will be light with temperatures reaching 16°C.

2 Look at the following photograph. Think of at least two captions that could be used to give this photograph different meanings.

Test *yourself*

Examine the advertisement on the following page closely.

Copy and complete the following sentences to help you write about the main *presentational devices* used in the advertisement:

1 This advertisement is trying to ....

2 The type of people who would read it are ....

3 The main colours used are ....

4 These colours make it look ....

5 The headline is ....

6 At the top left there are pictures which show ....

7 These pictures are meant to make you think that ....

8 The central picture is of ....

9 He looks ....

10 To the right of the page there are three pictures. These show you three different scenes from ....

11 Different colour fonts are used. The colours used are ....

12 These colours help to ....

13 Some of the words such as .... are written in capital letters. This makes them ....

14 At the bottom of the advert there is a strip of red with a series of .... These are there to ....

15 Overall I think the presentation of this advertisement is .... because ....

"I WAS A 99 LB. BARBARIAN"
- Gothar of Gundria

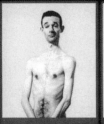
BEFORE UPGRADE

AFTER UPGRADE*

"I used to get molten lava kicked in my face. I was a little girly man, better suited to playing with sissy baby dolls than with battle axes. But then I mastered the UPGRADE FEATURE in BARBARIAN. Now nobody messes with me... NOBODY!!!"

"The 4-player mode is wicked. Now if I could just find 4 opponents I haven't already killed I would show you BARBARIAN's 8 character on-screen mayhem."

NEW & BETTER FORMULA
2/3 Brawl
1/3 Adventure

BARBARIAN is a revolutionary new game engineered to increase - and maintain - character power and ferociousness, fast! In recent head to head field tests, even mildly upgraded barbarians crushed their friends and foes without mercy. The MASSIVE 1-PLAYER QUEST mode - with 10 playable characters and hundreds of storyline branches - is the perfect training ground for customizing your barbarian, increasing strength and magic, winning friends and influencing people with pure brute force. But wait, that's not it, BARBARIAN also features an insane MULTIPLAYER MODE with up to 8 characters on screen at the same time, a totally interactive environment, and most of all the exclusive Save-your-customized-Barbarian-and-take-him-anywhere-with-you formula!

DON'T SETTLE FOR LESSER GAMES.
DEMAND BARBARIAN TODAY.

"Here I am getting Medieval on Keela. My weapon of choice is usually a tree, or a pillar, or my opponent... but you know me, everytime I can grab onto something and show off..."

"I had no social life before, but now, with BARBARIAN's SAVE AND RUN formula, I can take my muscles with me to a friend's... and work that disco magic, if you know what I mean..."

* Your actual results may vary, Mr. Saggy Breasts.

www.barbarian-game.com

3 Looking at language

Techniques writers use

Writers use many different techniques to create particular effects:

- sometimes they ask *questions* in order to make the reader think
- sometimes they *repeat* a particular word or phrase (group of words) for emphasis
- sometimes they *exaggerate* in order to make something sound very good or very bad.

Activity 1

Read the following texts. Identify and write down which of the three *techniques* each writer has used.

Text	Technique
A	repetation

A

FACT: nearly one in three 14 to 16-year-olds has taken drugs.

FACT: girls under 16 are smoking more cigarettes and taking higher quantities of drugs than boys of the same age.

FACT: one girl dies every month from sniffing solvents.

Sugar Magazine

B

For the most relaxing country cottage holidays, start with the most relaxing countries.

C

ques

IS YOUR BOYFRIEND AFRAID OF YOUR FATHER?

D exaggerate

Mega Fantastic Best Ever Sale Starts Saturday!

E

n o

SHOULD THE POLITICIANS TELL US MORE?

F f to

This is probably **the** worst film you could see this year. Marks for entertainment value – 0. Boredom rating – a massive, not to be beaten, 10 out of 10.

Persuasive language

Holiday brochures have two main purposes. They aim to:

- make the reader want to go to a particular place
- persuade the reader to choose that holiday rather than another one.

Activity 2

Read the following extract from a Butlins brochure. The annotations around the text help you to see how the words have been chosen to make the most of both the holiday and the company. Write the answers to **1** to **8**.

1 What does this phrase suggest? Where is it repeated?

6 The company's name is used often so the reader remembers it. How often is it used?

2 Repetition is used to emphasise the point. Find and list another two examples.

3 Suggests you won't find better. Find and copy one other phrase that also suggests this.

7 Adjectives are used to make the place sound good. Find and list three more adjectives in **this** paragraph that also do this.

THE TIME OF YOUR LIFE IS RIGHT HERE, RIGHT NOW ...

... AT BUTLINS!

At Butlins, fun is what we do best. It always has been. It always will be. That's why it's one of the UK's top destinations for family holidays and short breaks – all year round.

From appearances by kids TV characters to the latest chart-topping bands, the best in stand-up comedy and spectacular shows and musicals, it's all here for you to enjoy, day after day, night after night. That's what we mean by Butlins entertainment. But it's only part of the story.

Who could forget our brilliant Splash Waterworld centres and outdoor funfairs? And, with American pool, crazy golf and much more, the sport and leisure choice at Butlins is second to none. Add our great accommodation, bars and restaurants – all under one roof in three wonderful seaside locations – and you have the perfect recipe for an unforgettable holiday or short break any time of year.

Sounds appealing? Whether you're planning a break with the family, a partner or a group of friends, read on and choose it now. The time of your life is waiting for you at Butlins!

4 This suggests Butlins is like this all the time. Find and copy two other phrases that do this.

5 A list of three things is used to persuade. What are the three things?

8 A question is used to address the reader directly. In what other ways is the reader addressed directly in **this** paragraph?

Butlins brochure

Emotive language

Sometimes writers use words or phrases to make the reader feel a particular emotion, such as anger, sadness or disgust. This is called *emotive* use of language.

Activity 3

Read the following text closely. Copy and complete the chart below to show how the writer uses words to try and make the reader feel certain things:

Examples of emotive use of language	What the words suggest	What the writer wants the reader to feel
Children in Malawi face famine	*that children are going to starve because there is no food*	*concern*
food reserves are empty		*anxiety that things should be so bad*
Over 3 million people face starvation		
vulnerable children and families		
emergency food and other vital support		*we must act now in order to save lives*

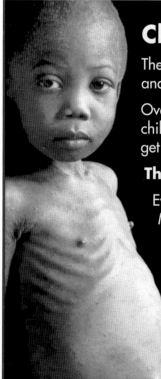

Children in Malawi face famine

There is little to eat. Adverse weather has caused a poor harvest and food reserves are empty.

Over 3 million people face starvation – many of these will be children and the elderly. If we do nothing, the situation will only get worse.

This tragedy can be avoided, but only if we act NOW.

EveryChild is working with vulnerable children and families in Malawi, providing emergency food and other vital support.

Your donation of £25 today could help families survive the famine. Please send a gift now.

Thank you.

Helping children worldwide

Registered Charity No. 1089879

EveryChild

More about technique

When looking at a writer's use of language you need to think about:
- the ways the words are being used
- the effect the writer wants to have on the reader.

In the extract on the opposite page the writer describes how Joe Louis, heavyweight champion of the world, defended his title against Max Schmeling.

Activity 4

1 Read the extract carefully. Copy the underlined words.
2 Match the underlined words to the correct description from the list below of what the writer is doing.
3 Check that you understand the match by answering the questions in italics.

a He uses a particular verb to give the reader an idea of how the fighter's fists moved. *Which verb?*

b He chooses a word to try and recreate a sound. *Which word?*

c He gives a list of adjectives to emphasise a point. *What are the adjectives?*

d He uses a metaphor to create a picture of what Louis was like. *What is the metaphor?*

e He uses this verb to suggest the crowd will never be able to forget what they have seen. *Which verb?*

f He uses language informally to give the impression he's talking directly to the reader. *Give an example.*

g He uses this image to show how badly Schmeling is beaten. *What image?*

h He describes the people watching as being in pain. *How does he show the pain? Why does he refer to them as 'It'?*

i He uses the present tense to make it feel as though it's happening now. *Give an example.*

4 Now think about the passage as a whole. Write two sentences to explain the effect the writer wants to have on the reader.

Explanations

metaphor – when a writer says something is something else.

1 <u>Listen to this, buddy,</u> for it comes from a guy **2** <u>whose palms are still wet, whose throat is still dry, and whose jaw is still agape</u> from the utter
5 shock of watching Joe Louis knock out Max Schmeling.

It was a shocking thing, that knockout – **3** <u>short, sharp, merciless, complete</u>. Louis was like this:
10 **4** <u>He was a big lean copper spring, tightened and retightened through weeks of training until he was one pregnant package of coiled venom.</u>

Schmeling hit that spring. **5** <u>He hit it</u>
15 <u>with a whistling right-hand punch</u> in the first minute of the fight – and the spring, tormented with tension, suddenly burst with one brazen spang of activity. **6** <u>Hard brown arms, propelling two unerring fists,</u> blurred 20 beneath the hot white candelabra of the ring lights. And Schmeling was in the path of them, **7** <u>a man caught in the whirring claws of a mad and feverish machine</u>. 25

The mob, biggest and most prosperous ever to see a fight in a ball yard, knew that here was the end before the thing had really started. **8** <u>It knew, so it stood up and howled</u> 30 <u>one long shriek.</u> People who had paid as much as $100 for their chairs didn't use them – except perhaps to stand on, **9** <u>the better to let the sight burn</u> <u>forever in their memories.</u> 35

Bob Considine, International News Service, 22 June 1938

Activity 5

The writer uses two *metaphors* to describe Louis. He says he was:
- a big lean copper spring (line 10)
- a mad and feverish machine (lines 24–5)

Choose three people from your family and friends. For each one, write your own metaphor to describe them, for example:

Kelly is a flash of lightning, *striking everything that stands in front of her.*

Test yourself

The following paragraphs continue the description of the Joe Louis fight.

1 The writer tells us there were four stages to the knockout. Work out where each of the four stages starts and ends. Write the line numbers of each stage, for example:

Stage 1: lines 1 to 4

2 Copy and complete the chart below. In the first column, write the phrases that are underlined in the extract. There are ten of them. In the second column, write about the way the writer is using words to produce a particular effect. The first two are done for you as an example.

Words the writer uses	How the writer uses words for effect
a lethal little left hook	*'Lethal' means deadly – 'little' suggests it's not his biggest punch – but it still hurts*
like a drunk hanging to a fence	*This simile ('like a …') shows how Schmeling reacts when he's hit – he's out of control and can't stand up without help.*
Louis swarmed over him	

There were four steps to Schmeling's knockout. A few seconds after he landed his only punch of the fight, Louis caught him with <u>a lethal little left hook</u> that drove him into the ropes so that his right arm was hooked over the top strand, <u>like a drunk hanging to a fence</u>. <u>Louis swarmed over</u>
5 <u>him</u> and hit with everything he had – until Referee Donovan pushed him away and counted one.

   <u>Schmeling staggered away from the ropes</u>, dazed and sick. <u>He looked</u> <u>drunkenly toward his corner</u>, and before he had turned his head back Louis was on him again, first with a left and then <u>that awe-provoking</u>
10 <u>right</u> that <u>made a crunching sound</u> when it hit the German's jaw. Max fell down, hurt and giddy, for a count of three.

   <u>He clawed his way up as if the night air were as thick as black water</u>, and Louis – <u>his nostrils like the mouth of a double-barrelled shotgun</u> – took a quiet lead and <u>let him have both barrels</u>.

4 Studying media texts

The media is the general term given to the different forms of mass communication. Examples of these include television, radio, cinema, the internet, newspapers and magazines. These are the forms of communication that reach large numbers of people in a short time. Each form is called a *medium*.

Advertisements

Advertising has an important role in the media. The designers of an advertisement might be trying to:

- sell a product or a lifestyle
- remind the reader of a particular brand name
- raise awareness of something that is happening
- persuade the reader to act or think in a particular way.

In order to get their message across, advertisers need to attract and keep their readers' attention.

When reading media texts you need to *read the images* as well as the words. Look closely at the poster on the following page. It is part of a charity's advertising campaign.

Activity 1

1 Discuss with a partner what you see when you first look at this poster. Make a note of your first impressions.

2 Now look more carefully at the detail of the image. Complete this chart by making notes about the details that you have noticed.

Figure on the settee	Man behind her	Background detail
Child's body – girl – wearing white vest – arms folded across body – long dark hair …		

3 Write two sentences about each of the following:
- what you think the image is trying to show you
- how you feel about this image.

Abuse through prostitution
STEALS CHILDREN'S LIVES.

Help end this obscenity. www.barnardos.org.uk 0845 458 0653

Barnardo's
GIVING CHILDREN BACK THEIR FUTURE

Now read the writing on the poster.

1 How does the *headline* '**Abuse through prostitution STEALS CHILDREN'S LIVES**' help to give meaning to (*anchor*) the picture?

2 Why do you think the words '**STEALS CHILDREN'S LIVES**' are in capital letters? Explain the connection between these words and the face of the child on the settee.

3 Look at the Barnardo's *logo*. What does it represent? How does it reflect the work of Barnardo's?

4 What is Barnardo's *slogan*? What is the link between the headline and the slogan?

5 Read the appeal to the reader at the bottom of the poster. What different things do you think this advertising campaign is trying to achieve?

Newspapers

There are *two* different types of newspapers:

- *national* newspapers which are sold in all parts of the country
- *local* newspapers which are only sold in one area of the country.

Newspapers appear in two different forms:

Tabloids: these are newspapers printed on smaller sheets of paper. They are thought to deal with less serious issues.

Broadsheets: these are newspapers printed on large sheets of paper. They are thought to deal with more serious issues.

Make a list of all the newspapers you can name. Say whether they are:

- national or local
- tabloid or broadsheet.

The front page of a newspaper has several identifiable features. Look at the front page of the *Daily Telegraph* on the page opposite and answer the questions in Activity 4.

Match the features listed below to the arrow numbers around the front page.

Photograph: this is there to grab attention. It may, or may not, be linked to the main story and is often in colour. *3*

Caption: the words below a photograph which give it meaning. *4*

Banner headline: main statement which spans the full width of the page. *9*

Byline: name of the writer of the article. *7*

Masthead: the title block which includes the name of the newspaper. *1*

Pugs: the areas at the top left and top right of the page. They attract the reader's eye and are used to show the date, price etc. *2*

Strapline: an introductory statement just below the main headline. *8*

Standfirst: the first paragraph of a report. It may be in bold print and/or the first word(s) may be in capital letters. *6*

Splash: the main story on the front page. *5*

Newspaper reports

Journalists are trained to write reports in a particular way. In their reports they usually answer at least five different questions. These are sometimes called *the five Ws*:

- **W**ho is the story about?
- **W**hat is the story about?
- **W**here did the story take place?
- **W**hen did the story happen?
- **W**hy is the story news?

The Daily Telegraph

No 45,809 **

www.telegraph.co.uk

Britain's biggest-selling quality daily

Monday, September 23, 2002 55p

407,791 voices cry freedom

When the country march ended at 5.38pm yesterday, it had become the biggest civil liberties protest in British history. **Stephen Robinson** was there

IT STARTED so quietly that at first one wondered if it was all going to be an embarrassing flop. At 7am yesterday the only people visible on the streets of central London were hundreds of police, closing roads and putting up tape and barriers.

In the clubs of St James's, unusually full for a weekend, the grander marchers breakfasted heartily. Some way away at the mainline railway stations, chartered trains were hauling the countryside to the town, and under the streets the marchers were making their way by Tube to the mustering points for the two marches, at Blackfriars for Livelihood, Hyde Park for Liberty, depending on where you had travelled from.

But early on the mobilisation was invisible to most Londoners, and it was only when you walked down Park Lane to the starting point of the Liberty march in Hyde Park that the sheer scale of the event became obvious. One minute it seemed like another late summer Sunday in London; the next the huge banks of people came into view, backed deeply into the normally vacant green acres of the park.

There was a palpable sense of excitement that something big was afoot. Most of the crowd queued for three or four hours before they could actually begin their march.

At the head of the Liberty march, a couple of activists

from the Union of Country Sports Workers, loudly denouncing the Countryside Alliance "and their establishment friends", demanded to march at the front of the Liberty rally, but the alliance's press officers wanted cute 12-month-old Sophie Large in her pushchair, with her camera-friendly placard: "When I grow up I want to go hunting with my Daddy."

After a certain awkward negotiation, the pushchair prevailed.

The placards, swaying in the sunshine, conveyed an attitude of defiance. "We will not be culturally cleansed", read one; "Future Criminal" read another carried by an eight-year-old; "Revolting Peasant" another, carried by an adult, dressed in the Sloane Ranger's weekend uniform of plum-coloured corduroys.

Then, at precisely 10am, with whistles, horns and bagpipes blaring, the Liberty march began to roll from the eastern corner of Hyde Park, and into Piccadilly.

Kate Hoey, the Labour MP and darling for many of the marchers for her brave and lonely stance within her party, stood at the front, alongside Richard Burge, the alliance's chief executive.

Mr Burge held his hands aloft, clapping the supporters who lined the route, in the way a footballer extravagantly applauds the terraces as he leaves the pitch, to show he is not cross about being substituted. One placard read: "Hoey for Prime Minister".

The crowd eased forward at

about half normal walking pace, into Piccadilly and past the Ritz where Londoners lined the pavement, shouting their support.

The marchers cheered one placard at the Ritz: "Kiwis Support Country Poms", carried by John Falloon, a New Zealand farmer visiting friends in England. Hunting is popular in New Zealand, and Mr Falloon said he worried that a ban in Britain might have a knock-on effect in his country.

As the giant procession snaked rightwards into St James's, the gentleman's clubs had all opened up. At Boodle's, the staff stood on the first floor balcony in their waiter's uniforms, quietly applauding the marchers.

The marchers loved that touch. Most of the the upmarket St James's traders were closed, but they had left banners of encouragement in their windows.

On surged the crowd, down Pall Mall, and into Trafalgar Square, where Mayor Ken Livingstone, no friend of the countryside or hunting, had left his mark.

The road narrowed into an uncomfortable funnel because of the continuing roadworks, forcing the marchers to furl their giant Liberty & Livelihood banner, as they eased around the construction equipment of the mayor's half-finished pedestrianisation scheme.

The Liberty march turned into Whitehall where – with immaculate timing – it merged with the Livelihood march which had been making its way over from its eastern starting point.

There were whistles and cheers and shouts of recognition as these two tributaries met in the middle of Whitehall to form a giant river of humanity heading towards the Cenotaph, where the marchers fell silent as a mark of respect.

This meant the marchers could not shout their true feelings towards Downing Street, which was just as well as the mood was specifically hostile to the Prime Minister. One man, dressed as the grim reaper with a Tony Blair mask, was wildly cheered.

If the well-heeled of St James's were sending their best wishes, the tone of the march was not at all grand. Early yesterday, a presenter on Radio Five Live put on a jokey posh accent as he spoke to a reporter in Hyde Park, perhaps to convey the BBC's general disdain for the event.

The presenter should have spoken to Mike Idle and Ewan Gaskell, keen members of the Ullswater fell pack, whose Cumbrian accents were so thick they warned "you might need an interpreter to interview us". Both had been to London only twice before, to attend the previous countryside marches, and they were only too happy to come back.

They said they were incensed that the media always suggested hunting was for rich people on horseback. "There are no toffs in our hunt," said Mr Gaskell, a van driver, rather giving the impression that they would not be welcome there. "And I'll tell you now, we're not going to stop because of what Blair says. How are they going to stop it? They don't police the towns in Cumbria, so how will they police the hunts?"

There was a definite edge of defiance on the streets. From

Continued on Page 2

Whitehall is swamped as 400,000 countryside marchers converge on Parliament Square at the climax of the Liberty and Livelihood march which brought central London to a halt yesterday
Picture: JEFF GILBERT

German election on a knife edge as both sides claim victory

By TONY HELM
IN BERLIN

GERMANY'S general election was on a knife edge last night after voting projections gave the narrowest of leads to Chancellor Gerhard Schröder's coalition government.

But as votes in key seats were being counted late last night, their lead was not great enough to guarantee victory over his conservative rival, Edmund Stoiber.

Analysts said the outcome could rest on between one and five seats.

Mr Stoiber's alliance of Christian Democrats (CDU) and the Bavarian Christian Social Union (CSU) did better than expected, according to early exit polls, winning around 38·9 per cent while Mr Schröder's Social Democrats (SPD) were hovering around 38·1 per cent.

But a stunning performance by the SPD's coalition partners, the Greens, gave Mr Schröder's coalition a good chance of clinching a second four-year term, albeit with the smallest of majorities. Mr Stoiber, 60, widely criticised as

ineffectual during the campaign, declared victory despite not knowing if he would become the first chancellor from the southern state of Bavaria.

"We have won the election," he told triumphant party workers at the Konrad Adenauer House, the CDU's headquarters in Berlin.

"The great party of the centre is back again," he said. "It is the biggest parliamentary party. We will do the best that we can do with this extraordinary result." His centre-Right alliance was about four per

cent up on the last election. But their traditional partners in government, the pro-business Liberals (FDP), did worse than anticipated, gaining 7-5 per cent while the Social Democrats' coalition partners, the Greens, exceeded all expectations to gain 8-8 per cent.

This gave the Red-Green coalition 46·9 per cent of the vote and the CDU/CSU 46·4 per cent.

The post-Communists, the Party of Democrats Socialist (PDS) were at around 4·2 per cent, not enough for a proportional share of seats in

the Bundestag. Mr Schröder, disappointed by his own party's performance but buoyed by the Greens, said: "We have no reason to hide. We have a good prospect of continuing our work and we want to continue it.

"A majority is a majority and if we get it we will use it."

Ludwig Stiegler, parliamentary party leader of the SPD, was more confident about the chances of the coalition returning to power. "We want to keep governing," he said. "Gerhard Schröder remains chan-

cellor." Claudia Roth, co-leader of the Greens, told joyous party supporters: "We have fought to the last and it has apparently worked."

Herta Däubler-Gmelin, the SPD's justice minister, who caused controversy by comparing George Bush with Adolf Hitler last week, lost to a conservative in the state of Tübingen. But under proportional representation she will keep her seat.

Reports: Pages 14 & 15
Editorial Comment: Page 23

Journalists also organise reports in a particular way. This is sometimes called the *news triangle approach*:

The main idea and the vital information
The details, still important but not essential
The extra information helpful to the
story but which might need
to be cut because
there is no
space
left

Activity 5

Read the report that follows, taken from the **Guardian** newspaper: 'Sailor survives after four months adrift'.

1 Find and make a note of the answers to the five Ws:
- **W**ho is the story about?
- **W**hat is the story about?
- **W**here did the story take place?
- **W**hen did the story happen?
- **W**hy is the story news?

2 Look again at the *news triangle approach*. Divide the article into three parts, writing down the line numbers for each part.
Part 1: The main idea and the vital information
Part 2: The details, still important but not essential
Part 3: The extra information helpful to the story but which might need to be cut.

Sailor survives after four months adrift
Duncan Campbell in Los Angeles

A lone sailor has been rescued after drifting in the Pacific Ocean for four months with a broken mast in a survival story 5 being likened to that of Robinson Crusoe. The man, a Vietnamese immigrant, survived by living on seagull, turtle and rainwater.

Richard Van Pham, 62, told 10 rescuers that he set off on his 26- foot boat, the *Sea Breeze*, from Long Beach in southern California to make the 25-mile trip to Catalina island, a popular day out for local sailors. 15

But he ran into a storm which snapped his mast, he said. After his radio and outboard motor also broke down, he found the boat drifting south. 20

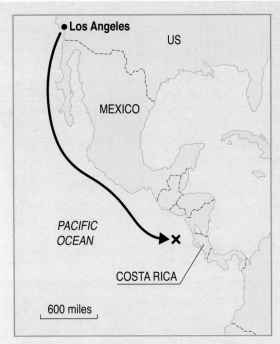

When he was rescued by the US Navy on September 17, Mr Pham had drifted 300 miles south-west of the coast of Costa Rica. By this time he had been at sea for four months, he said.

Mr Pham, who came to the US as an immigrant in 1976, had been living in his boat in a berth off Long Beach at the time of his trip.

A single man with no family, he had not told friends of his plans and so no alarm was raised when he failed to return after a planned day trip.

With only enough food for a day, he had to use survival skills to stay alive.

He collected rainwater in a five-gallon bucket and caught what fish he could. He nailed some of the fish to the boat to trap seabirds, which he roasted on a fire made from panelling ripped from the side of the boat. He trapped a sea turtle and then used salt from sea water to preserve it for days when he had caught no fish.

Staying under cover for most of the day to save himself from a blazing summer sun, he did have some entertainment: his solar-powered generator sometimes gave him enough power to operate his television so that he could watch videos he had on board.

But he had lost 40lbs from an already slim frame when he was finally seen by a US customs drugs spotting plane flying off the Costa Rica coast.

They alerted the US Navy and the USS *McClusky*, a guided missile frigate, went to investigate.

They were greeted by the sight of a lone sailor waving at them frantically.

'I see nothing,' Mr Pham told the *Los Angeles Times* of his ordeal. 'Then one day I see a plane.

'I know I'm close to people. They tip their wings to say hello. Two hours later a ship comes to my boat. I am very, very happy.'

The *McClusky* initially addressed him in Spanish but he responded in broken English.

He said he did not need medical treatment and merely asked the crew to help him fix his mast. After he had been persuaded that the boat was in such bad condition that it was not worth saving, Mr Pham reluctantly allowed the navy crew to sink it, going below deck so that he did not have to watch the boat being set on fire. He then travelled with the *McClusky* to Guatemala. The crew had a whipround on board to raise enough money for his $800 (£510) plane fare back to the US.

'The crew really adopted him,' said a navy spokesman. 'I think he's a very special man.'

Test *yourself*

You are going to study the media text on the page opposite in stages.

First, look only at the picture.

1 What does this picture tell you about:
   - the kind of work this person does
   - how this person feels about the work?

Now read the different things written on the firefighter's face.

2 What do these things tell you about:
   - the kind of work this person does
   - what it takes to be a firefighter?

3 The firefighter's name is written close to the picture. Give two suggestions as to why the advertisers included this.

Now read the writing in the two paragraphs.

4 How does the writer address the reader directly?

5 Re-read this sentence:

'But make it through our rigorous testing and you'll find it's a job that involves spending just as much time using that big grey muscle in your head as your triceps and hamstrings.'

In your own words, explain the point the writer is making.

6 The second paragraph starts with a list. By using this list, what is the writer trying to show the reader about this job?

7 Think about the whole advertisement. What different things do you think the London Fire Brigade is trying to achieve through it?

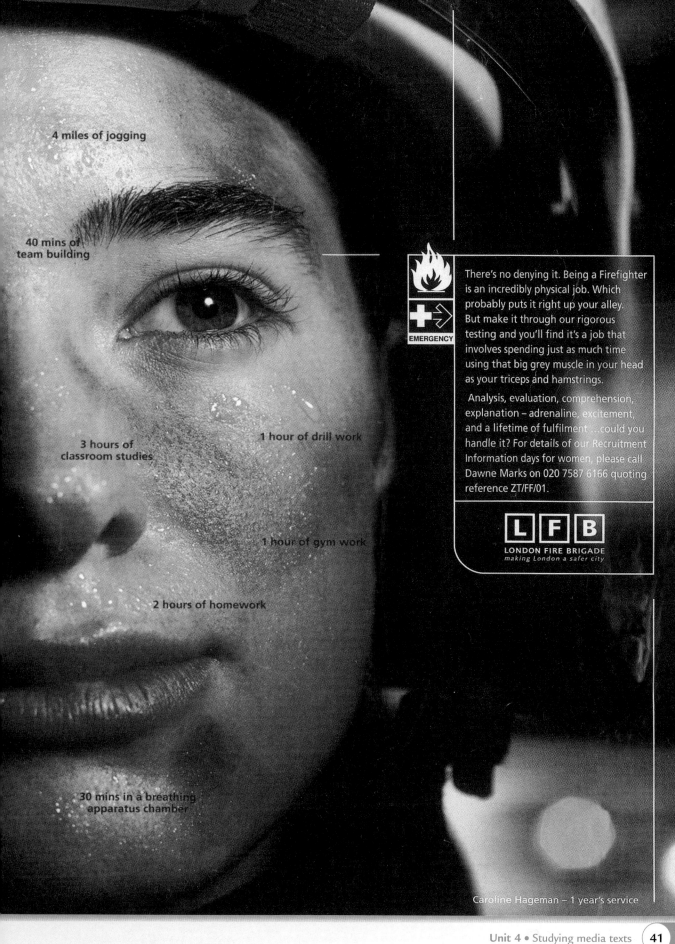

4 miles of jogging

40 mins of team building

3 hours of classroom studies

1 hour of drill work

1 hour of gym work

2 hours of homework

30 mins in a breathing apparatus chamber

EMERGENCY

There's no denying it. Being a Firefighter is an incredibly physical job. Which probably puts it right up your alley. But make it through our rigorous testing and you'll find it's a job that involves spending just as much time using that big grey muscle in your head as your triceps and hamstrings.

Analysis, evaluation, comprehension, explanation – adrenaline, excitement, and a lifetime of fulfilment ...could you handle it? For details of our Recruitment Information days for women, please call Dawne Marks on 020 7587 6166 quoting reference ZT/FF/01.

L F B
LONDON FIRE BRIGADE
making London a safer city

Caroline Hageman – 1 year's service

5 Choosing the right information

We read things in different ways, depending on:

- what we are reading
- why we are reading.

Skimming

Sometimes you need to read the whole of a text quickly to get a general idea of what it is about. For example, when you first look at a book you might read the blurb on the back to get an idea of what the book is about. This is called *skimming*, as you are only looking at surface details.

Activity 1

Skim the blurbs on the opposite page.

1 Which books would you choose to find out more about:
- the strange ways some people behave
- some of the world's unsolved mysteries
- stories that might frighten you.

2 Which book would you recommend to someone who liked to look at pictures?

Scanning

You don't always need to read the whole text. For example, when you read a timetable your eyes move quickly over the text until you see the key words you are looking for. This process is called *scanning*.

Activity 2

Look at the extract on page 44, which is from a leisure centre guide. See how quickly you can *scan* the text to find the answers to these questions:

1 What age of children does the crèche take?
2 What can you do on Wednesdays between 6.30 p.m. and 7.30 p.m.?
3 When is the Ladies Only session at the sauna?
4 Which class combines high rep weight training and aerobic conditioning?
5 How do you find out when reflexology is available?
6 Where will saver cards save you money?
7 Which fitness class is cheapest?
8 How many fast tanning sunbeds are there?

A What was the purpose of the ancient monument on Salisbury Plain known as Stonehenge? Why did thirteen people mysteriously die after the opening of Tutankhamen's tomb in 1923? In this book you will discover many strange and fascinating facts and opinions about some of the world's most intriguing mysteries from the past, which to this day remain unsolved.

Ancient Mysteries **by Rupert Matthews**

B Revealed within are some of the world's most baffling mysteries – from alien encounters and lost civilisations to fatal curses and unexplained jinxes. In lively and entertaining style, and with some 200 colour and black-and-white illustrations, this book's spread-by-spread storyboards provide readers of all ages with a fascinating introduction to some of the greatest earthly and unearthly enigmas.

Mysterious Facts

C Do you stay at home on Friday the 13th? Do you believe in ghostly apparitions, vampires, poltergeists and other spook-tacular stories? Well, prepare to be scared!
In this chilling collection of *Young Telegraph Spine-Tingling Tales* we tiptoe into the world of the paranormal to witness a hair-raising array of spooky subjects. Explore the haunting evidence of the unexplained – if you <u>dare</u>!

Young Telegraph Spine Tingling Tales

D The world would not be the same without those outrageous and eccentric people who seem to break every rule and defy convention at every turn. From the extraordinary obsessions of multi-millionaire Howard Hughes and the weird life of the surrealist painter Salvador Dali, to the Japanese soldiers who refused to surrender for decades after the end of World War 2 and the insane antics of Rasputin, these are tales of men and women who have shocked, startled and bemused us with their outlandish behaviour and lifestyles.

Bizarre and Eccentric **by Nigel Blundell**

FITNESS
CLASSES

Aerobics

Up-beat exercise to music class designed to improve overall body tone and develop cardio-vascular fitness.

Tuesday 7.30pm - 8.30pm.

Price: £2.90

Boxercise Circuit

Boxing training routines without the lumps and bumps! Exercise adapted for group general fitness work outs.

Wednesday 6.30pm - 7.30pm.

Price: £2.90

Step Aerobics

High intensity but low impact total body conditioning work out. Emphasis on legs, hips and bums.

Monday 6.30pm - 7.30pm and Thursday 6.30pm - 7.30pm.

Price: £2.90

Total Body Workout

Low impact aerobic warm-up, followed by toning of bums, tums and thighs within aerobic-music circuit.

Thursday 10.15am - 11.15am.

Price: £2.70

Body Pump

A fitness programme combining high rep weight training and aerobic conditioning into one exercise programme. A simple, fun workout accessible to both men and women at every fitness level.

Wednesday 7.30pm - 8.30pm and Friday 12.30pm - 1.30pm.

Price: £2.90

Pilates

A new fitness programme focusing on the principles of body control, centering, precision, coordination and stamina.

Monday 7.30pm - 8.15pm and Thursday 11.15am - 12.00noon.

Price: £2.90

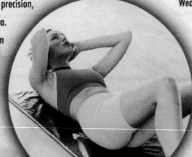

Sauna

Help ease the stresses and strains out of your daily routine by relaxing in our pine cabin. Cooling showers are available. Be sure to follow the cabin guidelines to maximise your enjoyment.

Opening times: Monday 12noon - 10.00pm,
Tuesday 12noon - 10.00pm,
Wednesday 12noon - 10.00pm,
Thursday 12noon - 10.00pm (Ladies Only 7.00pm - 8.30pm),
Friday 12noon - 9.00pm,
Sunday 8.30am - 4.00pm.

Price: £3.50 Adult (16+)
£1.85 Adult (16+) if after another activity.

Sunbeds

Two fast tanning sunbeds are available in their own individual rooms. Saver cards are available to save you money on maintaining your tan. Sessions are 15 minutes duration.

Opening times:
Monday to Thursday 7.30am - 9.40pm,
Friday 7.30am - 9.15pm, Saturday 8.30am - 6.50pm,
Sunday 7.30am - 8.50pm.

Price: £3.75 Fast Tan - Single,
£18.75 Fast Tan - Saver (6 visits)

Crèche

We operate a registered crèche service for children of customers, participating in one of our activities. The crèche caters for children up to the age of 5 and is operated at times co-ordinated with our activity programme.

Opening times:
Tuesday 11.45am - 1.15pm,
Wednesday 1.15pm - 2.45pm (8.45am - 10.15am School Holidays),
Thursday 10.00am - 12.15pm, Friday 12.10pm - 2.40pm.

Price: £1.30

Remedial Therapies

A selection of therapies including osteopathy, massage and reflexology are available at selected times.

Call 01609 778888.

Hambleton Leisure Centre

Looking across texts

Sometimes you will need to think and write about more than one text. You may be asked to:

- use material from two texts to build a wider picture
- write about the ways in which two texts are similar and/or different.

To do this you need to be able to take different pieces of information from different texts and use them together.

Activity 3

Read the following two texts: **Text A** and **Text B**.

1 Identify the *audience*, the *purpose* and the *form* of each text.
2 The key points from each text are listed in the chart below. Complete the key points by filling in the missing words.

Text A	Text B
• Young people are developing _a_ _Tipe B diabetes_. It's usually adults who get this.	• 72% of teenagers do less than _two hours_ of sport in school each week.
• Many 7–18 year olds are classified as _unactive_.	• Doctors predict huge rise in number of people with _heart disease_ disease
• Childhood obesity has _trebled_ in 20 years.	• Few people like doing PE in school because of _bad conditions_.
• Teenagers do less _PE_ in school than anywhere else in Europe.	• Sport in schools can be _exiting and worthwhile_.
• _Politicians_ are to blame for playing grounds being sold.	• French, German and Spanish do _3_ hours more sport per week and have _latest equipments and sports facilities_.
• France and _America_ treat sport in schools seriously.	• Sports fields are being sold by _local councils_.
• National _teams_ suffer because of this.	• Test results are more important than _health results_.

Children denied a sporting chance

In overweight, unfit, couch potato Britain, a disturbing new medical threat is emerging. For the first time, young people are developing Type 2 diabetes, a condition that until now has been found only in overweight adults.

What is happening is tragic but hardly surprising. Childhood obesity has trebled in 20 years. Almost all young people between 7 and 18 are classified as 'inactive'. Our teenagers do less PE in school than anywhere else in Europe.

And there is no doubt where most of the blame lies: with the politicians, who year after year promised to improve the state of sport in schools, but did nothing.

The rot began under the last Tory Government, when Ministers allowed councils to sell off school playing fields in their thousands.

Today, the situation is even more desperate. New Labour has broken its promise to stop the rot and the sale of playing fields continues. Plans to turn waste grounds into sports grounds have come to nothing.

Nobody can doubt the value of such facilities. France and America treat sport in schools with great seriousness because it promotes fitness and encourages discipline and teamwork. Yet in Britain, the politicians have made sure that organised games hardly exist in our state schools – with dismal consequences for our national teams in almost every sport, except rugby.

And now young people are being struck down by the diseases of middle age. The price of this folly is high indeed.

Daily Mail

Text B

20 ...

Dear Editor,

So, 72% of teenagers do less than the recommended two hours of sport in school per week and are becoming unfit, lazy and overweight. Because of this doctors are already predicting a huge rise in the number of people with heart disease. Who is to blame? Is it the teenagers themselves? I don't think so!

At my school we only get one hour of practical PE a week and by the time everyone's changed and registered that's down to about 40 minutes. We can't do PE if it's not on the timetable. Anyway, who wants to stand on a muddy field in the freezing cold carrying a battered piece of wood or kicking a piece of leather? Outdated showers that only spray iced water are the final straw!

But it needn't be like this. Sport in schools, *all* schools, can be exciting and worthwhile. It can offer choice and set a healthy pattern for adult life. Teenagers in France, Germany and Spain do on average 3 hours of sport per week *and* they have all the latest equipment, including sports centres and indoor pitches. What chance have we when our sports fields are being sold off to make local councils a quick buck and everyone's so concerned about test results no one has time for health results?

It's time for the government to raise our sports facilities to European standards *now*, before it's too late.

V. Rushton

Activity 4

1 Look back at the chart you completed in Activity 3. Compare the lists of key points. Talk about and highlight points which are:
   - similar
   - different.

2 Compare the two texts by completing the following sentences:
   a **Both** texts were written for the readers of a _____.
   b Text A is an editorial **but** Text B is a _____.
   c Text A is mainly about _____ **whereas** Text B is about
      _____.
   d Text A points to problems with Type 2 diabetes **but** Text B suggests problems
      with _____.

   The words in bold are used to make comparisons.

3 Now write two sentences of your own showing other similarities and/or differences between the texts.

Referring to the text

You need to refer to the details of a text to support the things you are saying. Sometimes you will refer to a detail, for example:

> *The writer of the letter argues that it is not the fault of the teenagers.*
> *He points out that in his school they only get one hour of practical PE each week.*

Sometimes you will quote directly from the text, for example:

> *He believes that one of the problems is that 'everyone's so concerned about test results no one has time for health results'.*

Notice how the quotation marks are placed before and after the words that are taken directly from the text.

Activity 5

1 Complete the following sentences by referring to details in the letter:
   a The writer tells us that teenagers in other European countries such as _____ get a better deal.
   b A rise in _____ is predicted because teenagers are so unfit.

2 Complete the following sentences by using quotations directly from the letter:
   a He believes that sport is worthwhile because '_____'.
   b He believes that sport is better for teenagers in other European countries because '_____'.

3 Write two sentences explaining who each writer thinks is to blame for what is happening to sport in schools. In each sentence use a quotation to support the point you make.

Test *yourself*

1 *Skim* the following four texts and answer these questions:

- Which text(s) would you read to find out about what foods you should eat?

- Which text(s) give you advice about exercises to do in winter?

- Which text(s) would you recommend to a friend who wanted to be fitter?

2 *Scan* the following four texts to find the answers to these questions:
- What does a balanced meal contain?

- What do you have to do in body sculpting?

- What racquet sports are recommended to Rachel Thompson?

- Who can eat a high-fat diet and still stay slim?

- What can eating too little lead to?

- What exercise is good for flexibility and relaxation?

3 Complete these sentences by comparing **Text A** and **Text D**.
- **Text A** tells you how to achieve a healthy diet whereas **Text D** _____.

- **Text D** tells you that athletes can stay slim on a high-fat diet but **Text A** suggests keeping fat content down by _____.

4 Refer to details in the texts to answer these questions:
- Why does Tee Dobinson in **Text C** recommend training with a partner?

- Why, according to **Text B**, should you make sure you get the right exercise class?

Highlight the details you have used in your answer.

A

Mind, Body & Soul   HOME SEARCH LINKS

Wired for Health

Healthy Eating

A healthy balance of foods provides the energy and nourishment you need to survive and to enjoy life. Eating too little can soon lead to illness, but eating too much or the wrong balance of foods can lead to problems too.

The Balance of Good Health makes healthier eating easier to understand. It shows types and proportions of foods you need to eat for a well-balanced and healthy diet. This balance could be achieved over a day, a few days or a week.

Balanced meals contain generous portions of starchy foods with plenty of vegetables, salad or fruit. Fat content is kept to a minimum by choosing low-fat or lean ingredients and by using low-fat cooking methods.

Why be active? / How much should I do? / What types of activity should I do? / One step beyond

B

Work it, girl!

If you've had a slobbed-out time you really feel to get going again. But if you're thinking of joining an exercise class, then make sure you get the right one, so you don't bust your guts too soon!

Exercise	Good for	What you have to do
Aerobics	Heart and lungs	Dance like a maniac and get toned up
Step	Heart, lungs, legs and bum	Like aerobics but you step on/off a block
Slide	Thighs, heart and lungs	Glide about on a board – very hard work!
Body Sculpting	Everywhere	Uses weights to tone up muscles
Circuit Training	Complete calorie burner	Loads of different exercises
Yoga	Flexibility and relaxation	Stretches and breathing contro.
Box Aerobics	Everything!	Boxing stuff...

Bliss Magazine

C

Q I spend a lot of time in the gym working out either on the rowing machine or treadmill, plus I normally jog first thing most mornings. I love exercising and I feel better for it, but now the weather has changed I don't feel like dragging myself outside. How can I keep up my enthusiasm?

Rachel Thompson

A Trying a different activity is always a great way to revitalise and remotivate. As an added benefit you may find that your current fitness levels improve too. If you don't fancy braving the weather for a while, what about an indoor sport like basketball, volleyball or any of the studio-based classes that come under the aerobic umbrella, like Body Pump or Spinning? Racquet sports like squash or badminton are great exercise, too. Phone around and find out what's available in your area, then keep trying until you find something you enjoy.

As you usually work out alone, see if you can arrange an exercise partner – training with a buddy can be fun and the fact that someone is expecting you can help to motivate you to make all your scheduled sessions.

TEE DOBINSON

Health & Fitness

D # Eat fat stay slim

Want to eat a diet that consists mainly of doughnuts and beer? Become a professional athlete. That's the message from studies in both America and South Africa, which have shown that not only will an athlete stay slim on a diet of up to 43 per cent fat, but that his performance might also improve. Unfortunately mere mortals are unable to expend the calories in the way endurance athletes can, so it's brown rice and vegetables for the rest of us.

Men's Health

Reading Poetry

For your GCSE examination in English you will be studying poems from different cultures and traditions. These poems are contained in your **AQA Anthology**.

In the examination you will be asked to show that you:
- know what the poems are about
- understand how the poet is using words to create a particular effect
- have thought carefully about the effect the poem has on you.

In order to do this, you need to study poems in particular ways. This section uses five poems from the **AQA Anthology** to teach you the skills you need. When you have completed this section, you should use these skills to help you study the other poems. It shows you how to:
- think about meaning
- look at structure
- explore language
- refer to the poems
- write about two poems.

Reading of poetry is tested in AQA A GCSE English, Paper 2 Section A.

What is culture?

The word *culture* is widely used. People talk about:

- a yob culture

- a youth culture

- a celebrity culture

- an American culture.

Talk about what *you* think is meant by the word *culture*.

Now read this dictionary definition of the word *culture*. ⟶

> **culture** (say **kul**cher) *noun* a general term for the huge range of ideas, knowledge and beliefs that are generally shared by the people of a country, race, religion or social group.

What are traditions?

Traditions are the customs that are particular to a culture. They are often handed down from one generation to another.

Activity ①

Choose a special time of year that is important to you and your family. It could be Christmas or Eid or Thanksgiving or another time.

Draw a spider diagram like the one here, outlining the different traditions you follow at this time of year – for example, leaving the presents under the Christmas tree.

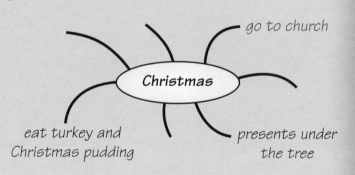

go to church

Christmas

eat turkey and Christmas pudding

presents under the tree

There are *poets* in every country of the world. Sometimes they write about things to do with their culture and traditions, that may seem strange to you. The poem might be set in a country you have not been to. The poets might write about people you have never seen and customs you have not experienced. They may use words you have not come across or used before.

Activity 2

1 Read the following poem carefully. It is set in an Indian village. In it the poet tells the story of what happened the night his mother was stung by a scorpion.

2 Look at these six pictures that show what is happening in the poem. Put the pictures in the correct order and write a caption for each one, for example:

> 1 = d. Scorpion gets ready
>   to sting mother

2c   3-a

3 The poem is divided into a long part and a short part. What happens in the short part? Why do you think the poet has placed this separately?

Night of the Scorpion

I remember the night my mother
was stung by a scorpion. Ten hours
of steady rain had driven him
to crawl beneath a sack of rice.
5   Parting with his poison – flash
of diabolic tail in the dark room –
he risked the rain again.
The peasants came like swarms of flies
and buzzed the name of God a hundred times
10   to paralyse the Evil One.
With candles and with lanterns
throwing giant scorpion shadows
on the mud-baked walls
they searched for him: he was not found.
15   They clicked their tongues.
With every movement that the scorpion made
his poison moved in Mother's blood, they said.
May he sit still, they said.
May the sins of your previous birth
20   be burned away tonight, they said.
May your suffering decrease
the misfortunes of your next birth, they said.
May the sum of evil
balanced in this unreal world
25   against the sum of good
become diminished by your pain.
May the poison purify your flesh
of desire, and your spirit of ambition,
they said, and they sat around
30   on the floor with my mother in the centre,
the peace of understanding on each face.
More candles, more lanterns, more neighbours,
more insects, and the endless rain.
My mother twisted through and through,
35   groaning on a mat.
My father, sceptic, rationalist,
trying every curse and blessing,
powder, mixture, herb and hybrid.
He even poured a little paraffin

40   upon the bitten toe and put a match to it.
        I watched the flame feeding on my mother.
        I watched the holy man perform his rites
        to tame the poison with an incantation.
        After twenty hours
45   it lost its sting.

        My mother only said
        Thank God the scorpion picked on me
        and spared my children.

Nissim Ezekiel

Explanations

diabolic: related to the devil
the Evil One: the devil
diminished: made less
purify: cleanse from sin
sceptic: person who doubts the truth
   of religion

rationalist: person who thinks logical thinking
   can explain everything
hybrid: a mixture of things
rites: actions in a religious ceremony
incantation: the saying of supposedly magic
   words

Activity 3

1 Re-read the poem. Copy and complete this chart by listing the things that tell you something about the place, the way the people live and the things they believe in.

About the place	How the people live	Things they believe in
rains for ten hours		

2 Use your notes from the chart to help you write a paragraph about the culture and traditions of the people in **Night of the Scorpion**.
You could start like this:

> From reading this poem I have found out many things
> about the place, the people and the things they believe in.
> It is a place where it rains ...

Accent and dialect

The words we use and the way we pronounce them reveals something about our culture. There are many different forms of English spoken across the world. People from Liverpool speak with a different *dialect* (the words that are used) and *accent* (the way the words are spoken) from people in Newcastle or Cornwall. People in America speak a different form of English from people in Jamaica – and from people in England.

Standard English is the form most often used in print (in newspapers, magazines and books) and in formal situations. Newsreaders on the television and radio generally read the news in standard English. Usually they do not have a strong regional *accent*. Why do you think this is?

In the following poem Tom Leonard, a Scottish poet, challenges the idea that the news should be read in standard English and without an accent. The words are spelt *phonetically*, which means as they are spoken. Try reading the poem aloud.

Activity 4

Copy and complete the following chart by writing what each word would be in standard English. A couple have been done for you.

Words in poem	Standard English	Words in poem	Standard English
thi		tokn	
wia		ma	
toktaboot		yirsellz	yourselves
wonna	one of	canny	

this is thi
six a clock
news thi
man said n
5   thi reason
a talk wia
BBC accent
iz coz yi
widny wahnt
10 mi ti talk
aboot thi
trooth wia
voice lik
wanna yoo
15 scruff. if
a toktaboot
thi trooth
lik wanna yoo
scruff yi
20 widny thingk
it wuz troo.
jist wonna yoo
scruff tokn.
thirza right
25 way ti spell
ana right way
ti tok it. this
is me tokn yir
right way a
30 spellin. this
is ma trooth
yooz doant no
thi trooth
yirsellz cawz
35 yi canny talk
right. this is
the six a clock
nyooz. belt up.

Tom Leonard

from **Unrelated Incidents**

Activity 5

1 What points do you think
   Tom Leonard is trying to
   make in this poem? Choose
   two or more from the
   following statements and give
   your reasons:
   - The news should be read in
     standard English.
   - The news should be read in
     the local dialect.
   - People who speak in a
     dialect cannot be trusted.
   - We should not judge
     people by the way they
     speak.
   - People look down on
     people who speak in a
     dialect.
   - People are more likely to
     believe someone who
     speaks in standard English.

2 Look back at the statements
   you have chosen. Do you
   agree with Tom Leonard's
   point of view? Give your
   reasons.

2 Thinking about meaning

When you read a poem, one of the first questions you need to answer is 'What is it about?'. Don't worry if you can't answer the question straight away. It may take several attempts before you understand what is being said. Often, the more times you read a poem the more layers of *meaning* you find in it.

First impressions

Read the following poem aloud twice. After you have read it twice, answer the questions on the right-hand side of the poem.

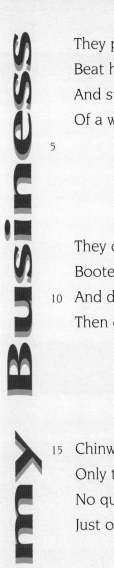
Not my Business

They picked Akanni up one morning   What happened to Akanni?
Beat him soft like clay
And stuffed him down the belly
Of a waiting jeep.
5   What business of mine is it   How did the speaker of the poem feel?
           So long they don't take the yam
           From my savouring mouth?

They came one night   What happened to Danladi?
Booted the whole house awake
10   And dragged Danladi out,
Then off to a lengthy absence.
           What business of mine is it   How did the speaker of the poem feel?
           So long they don't take the yam
           From my savouring mouth?

15   Chinwe went to work one day   What happened to Chinwe?
Only to find her job was gone:
No query, no warning, no probe –
Just one neat sack for a stainless record.
           What business of mine is it   How did the speaker of the poem feel?
20   So long they don't take the yam   Who do you think 'they' are?
           From my savouring mouth?

And then one evening   What happened to the speaker?
As I sat down to eat my yam
A knock on the door froze my hungry hand.
25   The jeep was waiting on my bewildered lawn
Waiting, waiting in its usual silence.   How do you think the
                                                speaker feels now?

Niyi Osundare

Explanations

Akanni, Danladi, Chinwe: African names
yam: a vegetable, like a sweet potato

Write two to three sentences which sum up what you think this poem is about.

Looking beneath the surface

So far you have thought about the surface meaning of the poem. Now you need to explore the other things the poet could be saying.

Activity **2**

1 Complete the following chart by showing:
   - whether you agree or disagree with the statement
   - the reason(s) for your decision.

Statement	Agree/ Disagree	Reason(s)
It's about violence in society.		
The poet is criticising people who don't help others.		
It shows that when you're hungry you can't risk standing up for your neighbours.		
It's set in a society where the people in power treat others unfairly.		
It's set in a country where people live in fear.		
Akanni, Danladi and Chinwe must all have done bad things.		
It shows that you have to look after yourself.		

2 The speaker seems to know Akanni, Danladi and Chinwe as he calls them by their names. What difference does this make to the way you feel about the speaker?

Now that you have started to explore the ideas in the poem you are ready to think again about the meaning of particular words and phrases. Re-read the first stanza of the poem and the notes that surround it:

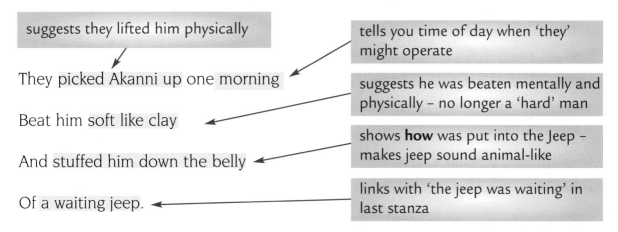

suggests they lifted him physically

tells you time of day when 'they' might operate

They picked Akanni up one morning

suggests he was beaten mentally and physically – no longer a 'hard' man

Beat him soft like clay

shows **how** was put into the Jeep – makes jeep sound animal-like

And stuffed him down the belly

links with 'the jeep was waiting' in last stanza

Of a waiting jeep.

Activity 3

Copy the first four lines of stanzas 2 and 3, and then make your own notes on what you can learn from the highlighted words.

They came one night
Booted the whole house awake
And dragged Danladi out,
Then off to a lengthy absence.

Chinwe went to work one day
Only to find her job was gone:
No query, no warning, no probe –
Just one neat sack for a stainless record.

What is this poem about?

Now that you have thought carefully about the poem, work through Activity 4.

Activity 4

1 Remind yourself of the work you have done in Activities 1, 2 and 3. Re-organise your ideas under two headings:

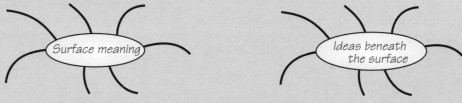

Surface meaning

Ideas beneath the surface

2 Now write two paragraphs about the meaning of the poem. You might find it helpful to use the following paragraph starters:

Paragraph 1: *On the surface 'Not my Business' seems to be about …*

Paragraph 2: *Having studied the poem carefully, I can find other meanings in it …*

Referring to the poem

When you write about poetry you need to refer to the poem(s). Sometimes you will want to refer to things in a poem without quoting directly from it, for example:

The poet, Niyi Osundare, writes about three people, Akanni, Danladi and Chinwe, who have all been badly treated.

At other times you will want to quote directly from a poem. These may be words or phrases, for example:

Akanni is beaten badly and 'stuffed' into 'a waiting jeep'.

Notice how the quotation marks are placed before and after the words that are taken directly from the poem.

Sometimes you will need to quote whole lines from a poem, for example:

The speaker, who has done nothing to help the others, finally becomes the victim:

'The jeep was waiting on my bewildered lawn

Waiting, waiting in its usual silence.'

Notice how:
- the lines of poetry are written as in the poem
- a colon : is used to show that the quotation is to follow.

Activity 5

1 Copy and complete the following sentences using suitable words or phrases from **Not my Business**:

   The speaker asks what business it is of his as long as no one takes the food from his '_____'.

   The violence with which 'they' treat people is shown with words such as '_____' and '_____'.

2 Copy and complete the following, using suitable words or phrases from **Not my Business**. Remember to use quotation marks.

   When Danladi is taken away he is dragged off to _____.

   When Chinwe goes to work she finds that _____.

3 Copy and complete the following paragraph by adding two colons and two sets of quotation marks. Highlight the punctuation you have added.

   The speaker shows he does not want to get involved when he says

   What business of mine is it

   So long they don't take the yam

   From my savouring mouth?

   In the end, however, he finds that he should have made it his business as now

   The jeep was waiting on my bewildered lawn

   Waiting, waiting in its usual silence.

3 Looking at structure

When we talk about the *structure* of a poem we mean:
- the way the poem is set out on the page
- the way the ideas are put together
- the links between one part of a poem and another.

In order to write about the structure you need to think about what the poet is trying to achieve by setting the words out in a particular way.

The structure of ideas

The following poem is about the experiences of slaves on the ships that transported them from Africa to the West Indies in the eighteenth century. The limbo is a dance in which the dancers pass under a stick by bending backwards. It is thought that the slaves used to limbo under the long iron bars to which they were chained in order to keep fit. To help the reader understand what the slaves went through, the poet focuses on one person – the 'me' who is the speaker of the poem.

Activity 1

Experiment with reading the poem on page 64 aloud. Decide:

- where to pause
- how quickly or slowly to read the words
- which words focus on the journey and which words focus on the dance
- whether some words should be read more quietly than others.

If you have a copy of the poem you could make a note of your decisions on it.

Activity 2

1 The following extracts have been taken from the poem. They show the experiences of the speaker. Put them in the correct order:

   a the drummer is calling me
   b the water surrounding me
   c the silence is over me
   d the darkness is over me
   e the music is saving me

   f the drummers are praising me
   g the dumb gods are raising me
   h the silence in front of me
   i the dark ground is under me

2 'In the poem the limbo dance represents the journey the slaves make.'
   Find three pieces of evidence from the poem that would support this statement.

LIMBO

And limbo stick is the silence in front of me
limbo

limbo
limbo like me
5 *limbo*
limbo like me

long dark night is the silence in front of me
limbo
limbo like me

10 stick hit sound
and the ship like it ready

stick hit sound
and the dark still steady

limbo
15 *limbo like me*

long dark deck and the water surrounding me
long dark deck and the silence is over me

limbo
limbo like me

20 stick is the whip
and the dark deck is slavery

stick is the whip
and the dark deck is slavery

limbo
25 *limbo like me*

drum stick knock
and the darkness is over me

knees spread wide
and the water is hiding

30 *limbo*
limbo like me

knees spread wide
and the dark ground is under me

down
35 down
down

and the drummer is calling me

limbo
limbo like me

40 sun coming up
and the drummers are praising me

out of the dark
and the dumb gods are raising me

up
45 up
up

and the music is saving me

hot
slow
50 step

on the burning ground.

Edward Kamau Brathwaite

Rhythm

The best way to understand *rhythm* is to think about beat. Rhythms are all around us.

1 Look closely at the picture below. Think about the different *sounds* and *rhythms* suggested by the things you see. Describe them.
2 Describe other familiar sounds and rhythms. It might help to start by thinking about water, machinery, etc.

When reading and writing about poetry you need to consider:
- the beat of the words
- the pattern of sounds they make.

Activity 4

Read the poem **Limbo** aloud again. Try tapping out the *rhythm* as you read it. How is the rhythm different to ordinary speech? Does it remind you of any particular sound?

Repetition

Poets often use *repetition* – when they repeat the same words or phrases (groups of words). They might do this in order to:
- strengthen the sense of a pattern, as in the chorus of a song
- to give emphasis to a particular word or idea.

Activity 5

1 Can you identify a chorus in the poem? Write down the words.
2 Give at least one reason why this chorus stops at line 39.
3 How many times does the word 'me' appear in the poem? Why do you think the poet uses it so often?
4 Copy and complete the following chart to:
- show some more examples of how the poet uses repetition
- suggest reasons why the poet uses repetition.

Words repeated	Lines where words repeated	Why the poet uses repetition
is the silence in front of me	Line 1, line 7	• *To emphasise the quiet* • *To compare the tension of facing the limbo stick with that of facing the long dark night that lies ahead*
stick hit sound		

Rhyme

Poetry is meant to be read aloud. It is the only way to feel the rhythms of the words and hear the patterns of sound. Some of these patterns can be heard in the *rhymes*. Words rhyme when they contain or end with the same sound. Rhyming words might be found:

- at the ends of lines
- within lines.

Poets can link ideas within a poem by using rhyme.

Activity 6

Copy the following extracts from the poem, then highlight the *rhyming words* in each extract.

a stick hit sound
and the ship like it ready

stick hit sound
and the dark still steady

b knees spread wide
and the water is hiding

c sun coming up
and the drummers are praising me

out of the dark
and the dumb gods are raising me

Poets use words in a variety of ways to achieve different effects. You need to be able to:
- identify how the poet is using words
- write about the ways the words work

Read the following poem about a Caribbean island man who now lives in London. The notes on the right-hand side will help you to understand it.

Island Man

(for a Caribbean island in London man who still wakes up to the sound of the sea)

Morning
and island man wakes up
to the sound of blue surf   As he wakes he hears the sea of his
in his head   island home.
5 the steady breaking and wombing

wild seabirds   In his mind he sees the birds and the
and fishermen pushing out to sea   fishermen of his island.
the sun surfacing defiantly
from the east
10 of his small emerald island
he always comes back   groggily groggily   He wakes slowly and reluctantly.

Comes back to sands
of a grey metallic soar
                              to surge of wheels   He hears the sound of London traffic.
15 to dull North Circular roar   The North Circular is a ring road around
                                                                              North London.

muffling muffling
his crumpled pillow waves   The dream of his island mixes with the
island man heaves himself   reality of London life.

Another London day   His life in London goes on.

Grace Nichols

1 Copy and complete the following chart by listing the things the island man connects with the island and the things he associates with London:

The island	London
the sound of blue surf	sands/ of a grey metallic soar
the steady breaking and wombing	

2 Your chart shows you that the poet presents the island and London very differently. Complete the following sentences by choosing the right phrase from the box below.

The poet writes about how the island man wakes to the sound of _____

whereas in London it is the _____ .

The island scenery is of _____ . In contrast to this the London scenery

is _____ .

> dull North Circular roar   wild seabirds and fishermen pushing out to sea
> blue surf in his head   sands of a grey metallic soar

Investigating words

When you are looking at language you need to think about how the poet uses words to create particular effects. For example, what is the difference between the effect of:

island man wakes up   (line 2)

and that of

island man heaves himself   (line 18)?

By identifying the effects you can work out why the poet uses different words. The first 'wakes up' suggests a natural waking while the second 'heaves himself' suggests that this is difficult and requires a big effort. The poet uses the verbs 'wakes' and 'heaves' to emphasise the difference in the way the island man feels about his homeland and London.

How do you think he feels about getting up in each place?

Copy and complete the following chart by:
- identifying the methods the poet is using
- suggesting why the poet has used words in these ways.

Words	The methods the poet uses	Why the poet has used words in these ways
the steady breaking and wombing	<ul><li>the regular rhythm – stea/dy, break/ing, womb/ing</li><li>the poet has made up the verb 'wombing' from the noun 'womb', where babies are conceived inside a woman's body</li></ul>	<ul><li>to give an impression of the regular sound of the sea</li><li>to give a sense of comfort and security and remind us that the island man is thinking of the place where he was born</li></ul>
the sun surfacing defiantly		
groggily groggily		
grey metallic soar		
surge of wheels		
dull North Circular roar		
his crumpled pillow waves		
Another London day		

Thinking about colour

Sometimes poets use *colour* in interesting ways to get across a particular idea. Colours are all around us. They affect us in different ways and we tend to associate or link colours with different things. Think about the colour white. What things are white?

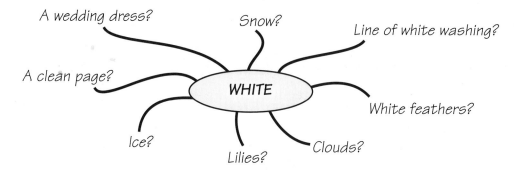

A wedding dress?

Snow?

Line of white washing?

A clean page?

WHITE

White feathers?

Ice?

Lilies?

Clouds?

In terms of ideas, white tends to be associated with innocence and purity and with a fresh start.

Activity 3

Grace Nichols uses three colours in **Island Man**:
- *blue* surf (line 3)
- small *emerald* isle (line 10)
- *grey* metallic soar (line 13)

1 Make three lists or spider diagrams of the feelings and things that *you* associate with each of these colours.

2 Suggest at least two reasons why the poet has chosen to use these different colours in her poem.

Listening to words

Poets often use the *sounds of words* to create certain effects. In the last unit you looked at the use of rhyme and repetition in **Limbo**. Read the following stanza aloud and look at the annotations to help you understand how the poet has used sound in **Island Man**.

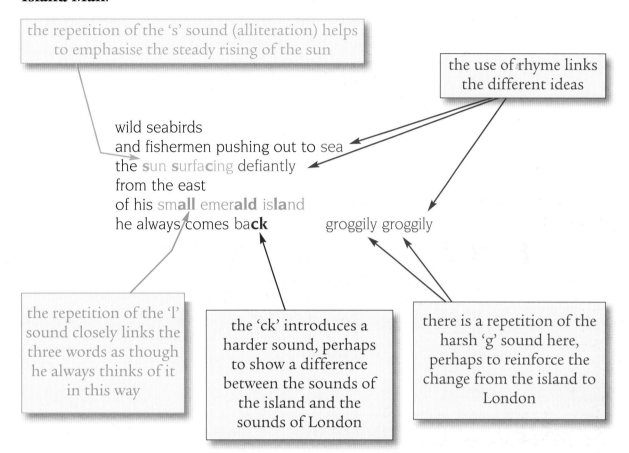

the repetition of the 's' sound (alliteration) helps to emphasise the steady rising of the sun

the use of rhyme links the different ideas

wild seabirds
and fishermen pushing out to sea
the sun surfacing defiantly
from the east
of his small emerald island
he always comes back   groggily groggily

the repetition of the 'l' sound closely links the three words as though he always thinks of it in this way

the 'ck' introduces a harder sound, perhaps to show a difference between the sounds of the island and the sounds of London

there is a repetition of the harsh 'g' sound here, perhaps to reinforce the change from the island to London

Activity 4

Poets often make use of *contrasting sounds*, for example:

> The whisper of a rumour
>
> The thud of schoolbag hard on desk.

1 Experiment with the use of sounds. Make two lists of words that you think have:
   - a hard sound
   - a soft sound.

   Say these words aloud to check their sound.

2 Now try writing a short poem, using some of the words you have listed to show a contrast in sounds. It could be about:
   - a football ground when full and when empty
   - a playground during break and after.

Writing about two poems

In your exam you will have a choice of *two* questions. You will have 45 minutes to plan and write your answer. You will be asked to write about at least two poems. The questions may name one poem and allow you to choose the other. You need to use what you know about both poems to answer the question.

Copy this sample question and follow Stages 1 to 4.

Compare what the poets show you about their cultures in **Night of the Scorpion** and one other poem. You should write about:
- the things you are shown
- how the poets organise their ideas to show you these things
- how the poets use words to show you these things
- what you think about each poem.

Stage 1

Highlight the key words in the question, for example:

Compare what the poets show you about their cultures in **Night of the Scorpion** and one other poem.

Now highlight the key words in the bullet points of the question.

Stage 2

Think about the poems you have studied in this book:

Night of the Scorpion (pages 54–55) **Limbo** (page 64)
from **Unrelated Incidents** (page 57) **Island Man** (page 69)
Not my Business (page 59)

They each show you something about the poet's culture. For this comparison we are going to compare **Night of the Scorpion** and **Not my Business**.

Write down the names of these two poems.
Find them in this book or in your Anthology and re-read them.

Stage 3

Spend about 5 minutes brainstorming ideas on both poems.
Below is an example of notes you might make for **Night of the Scorpion**.
The sub-headings match the bullet points in the question.
Complete the last section of these notes.

Night of the Scorpion

Things shown about culture:

Place – scorpions – heavy rains – mud huts – candles and lanterns –

peasants – superstitions – beliefs – holy man

How it's organised:

Like a story – told in first person – poet looking back at childhood –

very descriptive – lots of detail

How the poet uses words:

Makes scorpion seem both harmless and harmful: 'had driven him to

crawl' and 'flash of diabolic tail' – compares peasants to insects – like

swarms of flies (a simile) – suggests peasants were frightening: 'giant

scorpion shadows' – uses repetition to show how the peasants kept

talking: 'they said'

What I think about it:

Now make your own notes on **Not my Business**. Use the same four sub-headings.
This stage will take more than 5 minutes now, but in an exam, when you know the
poems well, 5 minutes should be long enough.

Stage 4

Use the notes you have made to help you write your answer. Follow this structure for your writing.

Start with **Night of the Scorpion**

Write about each bullet point in the order in which they are listed in the question.

Then write about Not my Business. Write about each bullet point in the order in which they appear in the question.

Remember to refer to details from the poems to support the things you say.

Remember to use quotations to support the things you say.

Helpful words to use when writing a comparison are:
also   but   whereas   however   the same as   different from   firstly

Lastly write about how the poems are similar and different.
You could point out that:

- they are set in different countries (India and Africa)
- they are both written in the first person as though from personal experience
- they are both about other people as well as the speaker
- they are organised differently on the page
- they both use repetition for effect
- **Night of the Scorpion** is about what happens when others come to help the mother
- **Not my Business** is about what happens when you do nothing to help.

Read through your work every ten minutes to check you are still focused on answering the question.

SECTION B WRITING

Writing

There are many different forms of writing. People write diaries, letters, notes, stories, poems, newspaper articles, leaflets and many other things.

Different kinds of writing require different skills and different levels of effort. A note written to a friend is written quickly, doesn't need much planning and is generally informal. In contrast, a letter to a would-be employer needs plenty of time, careful planning and is written in standard English.

It is important to match your writing to what is expected of it. When making notes, for example, you can waste time by writing in complete sentences. If you are asked to explain something and you end up writing a story, then you are wasting your reader's time. You need to be clear on what you are being asked to do and how to do it.

This section will help you to improve your writing skills. It gives you:

- examples of the different kinds of writing you will be asked to do in GCSE English
- advice on how to write for different purposes and audiences
- help on how to plan, sequence and develop your ideas.

Writing to argue, persuade or advise are tested in AQA GCSE English, Paper 1, Section B.

Writing to inform, explain or describe are tested in AQA GCSE English, Paper 2, Section B.

1 Writing for purpose and audience

When you write something it has:
- a purpose: the reason or reasons you are writing it
- an audience: the intended reader or readers for whom you are writing.

Activity 1

Read the following leaflet carefully and answer these questions:

1 What is the *purpose* of the leaflet? Is it:
- to make people vote
- to let people know they can vote
- to encourage people to register for voting?

2 What *audience* is the leaflet written for? Is it:
- adults who already have a vote
- 18-year-olds who are now old enough to vote
- 16–17-year-olds who will soon be able to vote
- adults who no longer use their vote?

Don't lose your VOTE

Why should I vote?

This country is a democracy. Every day, vital decisions affecting all our lives are taken by Members of Parliament and local councillors elected by the people. You can help choose them. Make sure you have your say – use your right to vote. If you don't, you will lose your chance to influence the way things are run in the country, or your part of it. All votes are equal – your vote is as important as anyone else's.

Can anyone vote?

No. You have to be 18 or over.
You must also be:
✗ a British citizen; or
✗ a citizen of another Commonwealth country; or
✗ a citizen of the Republic of Ireland; or
✗ for certain elections, a citizen of another European Union country.

Your name must be included on the register of electors, otherwise you can't vote.

How do I get on the register?

That's easy. Each year, at the end of the summer, the local Electoral Registration Officer (whose job is to compile the register) sends the electoral registration form (called Form A) to every household in his or her area.

If your household has not received the form by the middle of September contact the Electoral Registration Officer at your local council offices. Form A has to be filled in by one of the householders.

If you are a citizen of another European Union country, ask the Electoral Registration Officer for an application form.

✗ If you live in a hostel the form should be filled in by the people who run it.

✗ If you are a lodger in someone's house it should be filled in by the owner of the house.

✗ If you live in a flat with friends, one person should take responsibility for filling in the form.

✗ If you live on your own, in a bedsit for example, you should fill in the form.

Home Office Publications

We can usually identify *purpose and audience* by:

- what the writer says
- the way the writer uses words
- the way the writer presents the material.

Read the following *advice sheets*. They are both about drugs but they have different *purposes* and different *audiences*.

Text A

How to help a friend who has a problem with drugs

We all need friends. Sometimes we need the help they can give us. Sometimes it is our turn to help them out. If someone you know has a problem with drugs …

- ■ STICK BY THEM. DON'T TURN YOUR BACK ON THEM.
- ■ LISTEN TO THEM AND HOW THEY SAY THEY FEEL.
- ■ DON'T START SLAGGING THEM OFF TO THEIR FACE OR TO OTHER PEOPLE.
- ■ SUGGEST WHAT THEY MIGHT DO BUT DON'T KEEP ON ABOUT IT. THEY WILL HAVE TO MAKE THEIR OWN DECISIONS.
- ■ IF THEY WANT, OFFER TO GO WITH THEM IF THEY ARE GOING TO SEEK HELP FROM A DRUG AGENCY, DOCTOR, COUNSELLOR OR WHOEVER.
- ■ ENCOURAGE THEM TO BE POSITIVE ABOUT THEMSELVES.
- ■ ENCOURAGE THEM TO FEEL THEY CAN DO SOMETHING POSITIVE ABOUT THEIR PROBLEMS.

It can be hard work helping someone who has a problem with drugs. Then again it's not much fun for them and anyway what are mates for?

Text B

WHAT TO DO IN AN EMERGENCY

It is vitally important that you know what to do should the worst happen and you find your child drowsy or unconscious. It could save their life. Whatever you do, don't panic.

First make sure they've got plenty of fresh air.

Then turn them on to their side. Try not to leave them alone because if they are sick, they could inhale vomit.

Dial 999 and ask for an ambulance.

Collect up anything that seems to have been used in the drug taking – tablets, powders, solvents etc. – and give them to a member of the ambulance crew.

Health Education Authority

Activity 2

Copy and complete the chart by identifying:

- the *purposes* of **Texts A** and **B**
- the intended *audiences* of **Texts A** and **B**
- the clues in the words and presentation which helped you identify purpose and audience.

Text	Purpose	Audience	Clues
A			
B			

The writers of **Text A** and **Text B** use language differently to ta[...] [...]eir audience. In **Text A** we find phrases such as:

Stick by them

Don't start slagging them off

what are mates for?

The writer is using language *informally* to target a teenage audience. A *formal* version of each phrase would be:

Remain their friend.

Do not begin to criticise them.

what are friends for?

In contrast, **Text B** uses more formal phrases such as:

It is vitally important that …

should the worst happen…

The writer is using language *formally* to target an adult audience.

Activity 3

Write a short introduction to your school of about 100 words.

The *audience* for your introduction is parents of Year 6 pupils. Your purpose is to persuade them to send their child to your school. You should use language formally.

Here are some phrases you could use:

- *Your child will enjoy …*
- *There are opportunities to …*
- *Should there be any problems, …*

Targeting the purpose and the audience

When writing, you need to keep your *purpose* and *audience* firmly in your mind. Your writing:

- must achieve what you want it to
- must be relevant to your intended reader.

Read the following letter closely. It is written by a fireman to a newspaper. His *purposes* are to:

- inform his reader about what he does
- persuade the reader he is worth more money.

His *audience* is the readers of the newspaper. Read the letter and answer the questions that surround it.

Starts with a rhetorical question to draw in the reader. Where else does he use one?

Why does he repeat the word *life* three times?

How does he show the difficulties of his job?

Am I worth £30,000? In my career I have been taught skills to save life, prolong life and to know when to walk away when there is no life left. I have taken courses to fight fire from within, above and below. I can cut a car apart in minutes and I can educate your sons and daughters to save their own lives.

No matter what the emergency, I am part of a team that always comes when you call. I run in when all my instincts tell me to run away. I have faced death in cars with petrol pouring over me while the engine was ticking with the heat. I have lain on my back inside a house fire and watched the flames roar across the ceiling above me. I have climbed and I have crawled to save life and I have stood and wept while we buried a fellow firefighter.

I have been the target for yobs throwing stones and punches at me while I do my job. I have been the first person to intercept a parent who knows their son is in the car we are cutting up, and I know he is dead. I have served my time, damaged my body and seen things that I hope you never will. I have never said 'No, I'm more important than you', and walked away.

Am I worth £30k? Maybe now your answer is no. But when that drunk smashes into your car, or the candle burns down too low, or your child needs help, you will find I'm worth every last penny.

Jay Curson
Firefighter, Nottingham

Guardian

Speaks directly to the readers. What is he trying to get them to think about?

Repeats *I* and *I have* to show the range of things he does. How does he show the dangers of his job?

What point does he make in the last paragraph?

The writer of the letter targets *purpose* and *audience* through what he writes and the way that he writes it. He uses certain techniques.

- **Addresses reader directly**: The writer makes a direct contact with the reader by using the words 'you' and 'your', for example:

  No matter what the emergency, I am part of a team that always comes when you call.

- **Rhetorical questions**: These are questions that a writer puts to the readers to involve them and make them think, for example:

  Am I worth £30K?

- **Groups of three**: Often three items are grouped together to provide a fuller picture and to have more effect. Usually the most powerful idea or image is placed last for emphasis, for example:

  I have served my time, damaged my body and seen things that I hope you never will.

1 Re-read the letter. Give it a mark out of 5 for how well you think it targets:
   a purpose
   b audience.

1	2	3	4	5

not at all   **brilliantly**

Give a reason to explain each of your marks.

2 Write a letter to a newspaper suggesting that one of the following should be paid more:
   • a dinner lady
   • a school cleaner
   • a school caretaker.

Write your letter in the first person as though you were that person.

Your *purpose* is to persuade the readers of the newspaper that you are worth more money. Aim to:
   • give a range of reasons why you should be paid more
   • make direct contact with your reader
   • use a rhetorical question
   • use a group of three.

Writing *your own*

Read the extract below. It is taken from a holiday brochure. Its *purpose* is to persuade people to buy that holiday. Its *audience* is teenagers and young adults. Think about the methods the writer uses to persuade the reader.

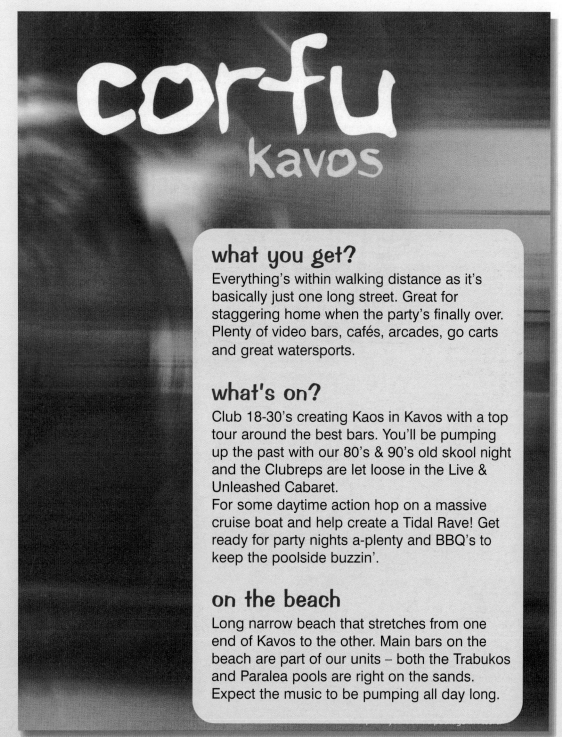

corfu
kavos

what you get?

Everything's within walking distance as it's basically just one long street. Great for staggering home when the party's finally over. Plenty of video bars, cafés, arcades, go carts and great watersports.

what's on?

Club 18-30's creating Kaos in Kavos with a top tour around the best bars. You'll be pumping up the past with our 80's & 90's old skool night and the Clubreps are let loose in the Live & Unleashed Cabaret.
For some daytime action hop on a massive cruise boat and help create a Tidal Rave! Get ready for party nights a-plenty and BBQ's to keep the poolside buzzin'.

on the beach

Long narrow beach that stretches from one end of Kavos to the other. Main bars on the beach are part of our units – both the Trabukos and Paralea pools are right on the sands. Expect the music to be pumping all day long.

Club 18-30

Now write the text for a holiday brochure for a place of your choice. Your purpose is to persuade people to go there on holiday. Your audience is teenagers and young adults.

Follow these stages:

Stage 1

Choose your place and brainstorm your ideas about it.

Stage 2

Organise your ideas around a series of sub-headings, for example:

• *Things to do*   • *Where can I stay?*   • *Bars, clubs and music*   • *What will it cost?*

Stage 3

Think about how you should use language to appeal to your audience. Look at the brochure for some clues on how to do this.

Stage 4

Write the text for your brochure. Use the present tense as you are writing about the place as it is now. Re-read your work at the end of each paragraph to check you are targeting purpose and audience.

2 Writing to argue

Key points

When you *write to argue* your aim is to present and develop a particular point of view. Letters to newspapers and magazines often present an argument. To do this the writer will make a number of *key points*.

A key point often appears near the start of a paragraph. It is then developed in the rest of the paragraph.

Read the following letter carefully:

HAVE YOUR SAY

It's time we got rid of school uniform. No one I know likes wearing it. It's old-fashioned, uncomfortable and not very practical. Pupils would be much happier if they could wear their own clothes to school and there would be far fewer silly arguments over why you haven't got a tie on or how many earrings you can wear. Just think of the time the teachers could save if they didn't have to check uniform.

It's not just that, though. Clothes are a way of expressing individuality. I choose my clothes to say something about the kind of person I am. Individuality is a good thing. We don't all want to grow up like sheep just following the leader, do we? Teachers are always telling us to take responsibility for ourselves. So why should we all have to wear the same clothes? It's not even as though we get to choose what the uniform should be. My school has had the same uniform ever since my oldest sister was here and she left ten years ago!

I've just finished school and finally I can throw my hated uniform in the bin. There's just one thing I intend to keep and that's the shirt I wore on the last day. It's covered in my friends' names and I shall keep it always. It's the only bit of my uniform I've ever taken pride in!

Karen, Nottingham

In the first paragraph of this letter the key point is developed in the following way:

KEY POINT
It's time we got rid of school uniform

- No one likes wearing it
- It's old-fashioned, uncomfortable, not practical.
- Pupils would be happier if they wore their own clothes.
- Fewer silly arguments.
- Teachers would save time.

1 Identify and write down the key point in the second paragraph.
2 List the other points that the writer makes in the second paragraph to develop this key point.

Techniques for writing to argue

To present the argument effectively, the writer uses several techniques.

Activity 2

Match the features of the writing listed in the first column to examples taken from the letter. The first two are done for you:

Features of writing	Examples from the letter
Makes clear opening statements.	'It's time we got rid of school uniform. No one I know likes wearing it.'
Tries to make the reader think this is a good idea.	'Pupils would be much happier if they could wear their own clothes to school.'
Moves on to a new point.	
Writes in the present tense.	
States opinion as fact.	
Uses 'we' to get the reader on her side.	
Uses rhetorical questions to make the reader think.	
Gives evidence from own experience to support argument.	
Uses an exclamation to emphasise a point.	

You are going to write a letter for the 'HAVE YOUR SAY' page of a magazine. Choose a subject you feel strongly about. It could be to do with school or something else, for example: 'Assemblies should be banned' or 'Footballers get paid too much'. Follow these stages:

- State what your subject is.
- Plan by listing:
  - **three** key points you want to make
  - the points you will make to develop these key points.
- Start each paragraph with a new key point.
- Write your letter using **at least four** of the features of writing to argue listed in Activity 2.
- Highlight and label the features of writing to argue that you have used.

Facts and figures

Sometimes writers support their arguments by using *facts* and *figures*. These can make an argument seem more powerful.

Read the following article closely. Identify and copy three *facts* based on *figures* which are used by the writer in the first two paragraphs.

Bullying:
is your child a victim?

Two in five school children are regularly being bullied. Anne Montague finds out who the bullies are – and how to stop their reign of terror.

The most recent study of 1,000 children aged between eight and 16, by Dr Peter Smith at the University of Sheffield, found that 20 per cent of them were bullied occasionally. Ten per cent of the children questioned had been bullied within the last week.

When Michele Elliott of Kidscape – an organisation founded to keep children safe from a variety of dangers including bullying – interviewed 4,000 children, she found that 38 per cent had been bullied badly enough to describe the experience as 'terrifying'. This situation can't be allowed to continue.

Why don't children tell?
It is perhaps because of the secrecy surrounding bullying that parents are the last to know. Bullying flourishes because the victim is not only vulnerable but bound by a code of 'honour' – 'it's wrong to tell tales'– and fear – 'don't tell or I'll hit you'. Other children won't tell, probably because they're afraid that they too will be bullied. We must try to break this code of silence.

In an exam you may need to make up 'facts' and 'figures' to support your argument. Imagine you have been asked to argue that more should be done to help children who commit crimes because of bullying.

Make up and list three 'facts and figures' that you could use to support your argument, for example: *'Three out of five children caught shoplifting last year said that bullies had forced them to do it.'*

Explanations

Re-read the last paragraph of **Bullying**. In order to move the argument forward, the writer makes suggestions that might explain the figures:

It is perhaps because of the secrecy surrounding bullying that parents are the last to know. (lines 24–27)

Other children won't tell, **probably because** they're afraid that they too will be bullied. (lines 32–35)

Other ways of introducing *explanations* include:
- This suggests that ...
- One possible explanation is that ...
- It may be because ...
- This could be as a result of ...

Think of and write down an explanation for each of the following statements. Use the sentence starter given to you:

1 Parents often don't realise their child is being bullied.
   This could be because ...

2 Children who are being bullied may well start to steal from their parents.
   One explanation for this is that ...

3 Some schools do very little to stop bullies.
   A possible reason for this is ...

4 Research shows that bullies are often unhappy children.
   This suggests that ...

Quotations

When writing to argue it often helps to introduce an expert's point of view. Read this extract taken from later in the **Bullying** article:

Bullying:
is your child a victim?

Bullying takes many different forms, although it nearly always happens in front of other children. Punching, kicking and gang attacks are commonplace. Bullies frequently lie in wait to 'ambush' their victim. Victims often have their clothes ripped, school books torn up, and their possessions stolen. 'Our interviews with children show that bullies don't understand other people's feelings or understand they're hurting other children,' says Valerie Besag, who's an educational psychologist.

The writer quotes the expert Valerie Besag to make the point that the bullies do not realise they are hurting other children. The words of Valerie Besag are placed within *quotation marks*.

Activity 7

In an exam you may need to make up '*quotations*' to support your argument.

Imagine you have been asked to argue that schools should do more to stop bullying. Copy and complete these sentences by giving the experts names and deciding what they say.

Head Teacher, _____(name)_____, said '_____(quotation) _____:

Year 7 pupil, _____(name)_____, said '_____(quotation) _____:

_____, mother of the bullied child, said '_____(quotation) _____:

Writing *your own*

Your local newspaper is running a competition, looking for the best and most original articles on **How we should improve our area**.

Write an article in which you argue for particular improvements. Your audience is the readers of your local newspaper. Your purpose is to argue in favour of a particular idea or ideas.

Follow these **five** planning stages:

Stage 1

First you need the *idea(s)*. Here are some suggestions to think about:
- providing better sports/leisure facilities
- improving transport
- knocking down a derelict area and replacing it with a park
- tackling specific problems such as drug abuse or litter.

Write down how you think your area could be improved.

Stage 2

List the *key points* you want to make about:
- why your area needs what you suggest
- the difference it would make to your area.

Stage 3

List the points that other people might make against your suggestion, for example:
- 'What about the cost?'
- 'It's not practical.'
- 'Only a few people would benefit.'

Make a note of how you would answer them.

Stage 4

List the *facts* and *figures* you could use. Remember, you can make them up.
What experts could you quote? Name them and decide what they say.

Stage 5

You are now ready to write your article. Here is a possible order for you to follow:
- what your area needs and why
- how this could be achieved
- the objections people might make and how you would answer them
- the advantages your idea(s) would bring.

When you have finished each paragraph, read through your writing. Have you covered all your key points? Is your argument clear? Will you convince your readers?

3 Writing to persuade

When you are *writing to persuade*, your aim is to make your reader believe something, agree with something or do something. You need to work hard to get them on your side.

Activity 1

Read the following two letters, **A** and **B**. Think about:

- what is said
- how it is said.

List the reasons why **B** is more likely to persuade than **A**.

A

Dear Aunty Joan,
Can I come and stay at your house over the summer holidays? Mum and Dad are going to Spain for two weeks and want me to stay at Gran's but it's boring there. I said I'd prefer to stay with you. Can you let Mum know if it's all right?
Love,
Chris

B

Dear Aunty Joan,
Please can I come and stay with you in the summer holidays? Mum and Dad are off to Spain for two weeks and I'll be left on my own. Mum wants me to go to Gran's, which is okay, but I'd much rather come and stay with you. It's ages since I last saw you and I've got lots of news to tell you.
    Don't worry about me getting in the way. I'm good at looking after myself and I can even cook a few meals. Delicious! Now I'm fifteen there's no reason I shouldn't be able to babysit for Emma and Jude, if you and Mike want a night on the town. I've done quite a bit of babysitting so you needn't fear. Ring me if there's anything you need to ask.
Please say yes.

Love,
Chris

You are taking part in a sponsored three-mile run for a charity of your choice. Write a letter to a relative asking them to sponsor you. Your aim is to raise as much money as you can. Aim to:

- give details of the run and the charity
- sound enthusiastic and friendly
- tell them you will be in touch after the run.

Techniques for writing to persuade

Writers use a range of techniques when writing to persuade. The writer of the following charity letter hopes to persuade the readers to donate money to help the homeless.

Activity 3

Read the following letter closely. The following annotations describe the techniques the writer is using. Match these annotations to the numbers in the letter:

a Rhetorical question used to draw the reader in.
b Group of three used to give extra impact.
c Addresses the reader directly as 'you'.
d Repeats the idea that they can save lives.
e Gives evidence to support the opening statement.
f Short sentence used to give extra impact.
g Clear statement of what Shelter hopes to achieve.
h Words are repeated to emphasise the message.
i Direct, dramatic opening statement, intended to grab the reader's attention.
j Uses 'we' to create the sense of Shelter working with its supporters.

Will the next person you see sleeping rough still be alive in the morning?

1

Dear Reader,

2 Make no mistake, life on the streets really does kill. I have seen it time after time. During one of the last severely cold spells Shelter workers found a man sleeping rough who had frostbite. **3** He died before they got him to hospital. Nobody knew **4** his name.

Think of it. Dying cold, hungry and alone. **5**

This cruel vision - homeless people lying dead on the streets from the cold - is why Shelter has launched its Winter Nights appeal.

6 Our aim is to help set up a network of emergency overnight accommodation across the country in schools, churches and hospitals - during those bleak, freezing months.

Just as important, we must gear up Shelter's nationwide network of advice services to help ensure that cold and hungry people, wherever they are, can find the closest available bed for the night.

7 **So I'm writing to ask you if you can make a gift. Something which will help stop homeless people dying on our streets this winter.**

With temperatures at the lowest of the year, the cold and the rain take a harsh toll on bodies already weakened by poor nutrition. All over the country homeless people are in desperate need of warmth, food and shelter.

8 Changes are desperately needed.

Your help is desperately needed.

9 Our aim is to make thousands of bed spaces available nationwide during the harshest weather. Can you help Shelter meet the need? We mustn't let people die, cold and homeless, on the streets.

10 **Your gift to the Winter Night's appeal could help save lives.**

Read the account below of Janice.

Using the information given here and your own ideas, write a short appeal. Your *audience* is the readers of a teenage magazine. Your *purpose* is to persuade them to give money to help young people like Janice. You could start your appeal with the question '**Can You Help Janice?**'

Aim to use at least four of the techniques of writing to persuade that you identified in Activity 3.

A quarter of people living rough are aged 25 or under

Janice

Her parents broke up when she was ten. Her mum's new boyfriend began to beat her. And at fourteen, when his sexual abuse wouldn't stop, she ran away.

Janice has spent a third of her life living rough. She's been beaten up in back alleys and sexually assaulted so often she doesn't even want to talk about it. Sitting in shop doorways, all Janice can think about is how much she wants to die.

Shelter/Crisis Winterwatch Survey

How writers use words to persuade

An important feature of *writing to persuade* is the way writers use words to appeal to the reader. Sometimes a writer will try to make the reader feel something. This is known as *emotive use of language*. Look at the following:

> Think of it. Dying cold, hungry and alone.
> This cruel vision – homeless people lying dead on the streets from the cold – is why Shelter has launched its Winter Nights appeal.

The words are simple and to the point. They invite the reader to think of what it must be like to die in this way. The build-up of adjectives: '*cold, hungry and alone*' create a picture in the mind of the reader. The word '*cruel*' emphasises how awful this is and this is reinforced by the idea of the '*homeless people lying dead on the streets from the cold*'.

The writer is trying to convince the reader that:
- this is terrible
- they must do something to help change it.

Activity 5

According to Shelter, the number of young people under the age of 16 who are living on the streets is rising.

1 Write three sentences about this. Aim to convince your readers that this is terrible by using language *emotively*. Here are some words you could use:

> appalling   disgraceful   pitiful   desperate   an outrage
>
> vulnerable children   all alone   victims   shocking

2 When you have finished your three sentences, underline the words which show you have used language emotively.

Writing *your own*

Write a letter to the Governors of your school. Your aim is to persuade them to give the profits from a school concert to the charity of your choice.

Follow these stages:

Stage 1

- Choose a charity that you know something about.
- List the reasons why your charity is worth supporting.
- List examples of the work your charity does. These can be made up.

Stage 2

Decide how you are going to organise your material. You could:
- start by stating what you want the governors to do
- go on to give several clear reasons why your charity is worth supporting
- end by restating what you want and encouraging the Governors to give their support.

Stage 3

Think about and make notes on the ways you could use:
- rhetorical questions to make your readers think
- personal evidence to support the points you make
- repetition to give your words more effect
- emotive language to touch the feelings of your readers.

Stage 4

Write your letter. When writing a formal letter, set it out in the following way:

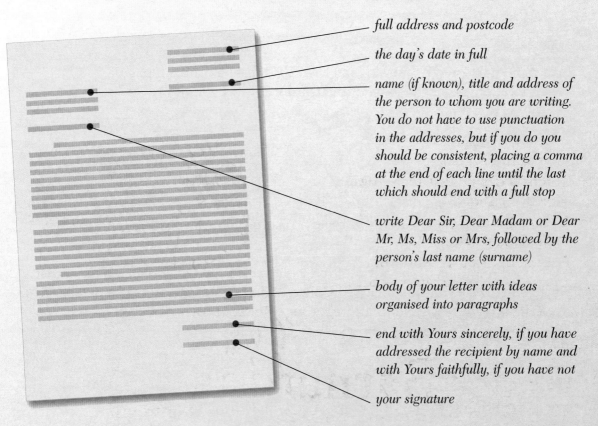

full address and postcode

the day's date in full

name (if known), title and address of the person to whom you are writing. You do not have to use punctuation in the addresses, but if you do you should be consistent, placing a comma at the end of each line until the last which should end with a full stop

write Dear Sir, Dear Madam or Dear Mr, Ms, Miss or Mrs, followed by the person's last name (surname)

body of your letter with ideas organised into paragraphs

end with Yours sincerely, if you have addressed the recipient by name and with Yours faithfully, if you have not

your signature

Stage 5

When you have finished each paragraph, read through your writing. Are your ideas expressed clearly? Could you make it more persuasive? Finally, don't forget to sign your letter!

4 Writing to advise

When you *write to advise*, your aim is to offer suggestions that will help to solve a particular problem. You find advice in newspapers, advertisements, leaflets, books, on the net and also in the problem pages of magazines.

Using different types of verbs

You will often find the following types of *verbs* in writing to advise.

Imperatives

These are *verbs* which can be used to tell the reader what to do, for example:
- **Have** a word with the ring leader.
- Before you get involved, **ask** your sister how she feels and **see** if she'd welcome your input. If she does want help, **talk** to the girls.

Modal verbs

There are *nine verbs* in this group:

> can, could, may, might, will, would, shall, should, must

These are verbs which suggest possibilities. They can only be used with another verb, for example:
- Starting a new school **can** be difficult.
- Explain it's great if they want to be mates with your sis' but if they don't, they **should** take a back seat so she **can** start making friends with people who really like her.

your life sorted

I'm very worried about my younger sister. She recently started at my school and I've noticed three of her so-called friends ignoring her and leaving her on her own all the time. She doesn't know what she's done wrong and it's upsetting her. Should I get involved?

Concerned, 15, Gloucestershire

> Uses present tense to show understanding that it's a current problem

> Gives further explanation

> Addresses reader directly to make it personal

MATTHEW SAYS: Starting a new school can be difficult. It's a time of change and making adjustments to a new place and new people. It's understandable that you're worried and good to know you're looking out for your younger sister. If these girls are deliberately making her life difficult, it's bullying. Have a word with the ring leader. Explain it's great if they want to be mates with your sis' but if they don't, they should take a back seat so she can start making friends with people who really like her.

ANDREA SAYS: Before you get involved, ask your sister how she feels and see if she'd welcome your input. If she does want help, talk to the girls. But, if this doesn't work, your parents need to contact staff at school. The important thing is not to ignore what's going on. It won't just go away and could lead to more serious problems. For information on dealing with bullying contact the **Kidscape campaign for Children's Safety on 020-7730 3300 or www.kidscape.org.uk**

Bliss magazine

> Uses non-standard English to be informal and friendly

> Makes helpful suggestion

> Gives a warning

> Gives other contacts

Activity 2

Read the extract on the following page from another problem page. Copy and complete this chart by identifying the different uses of *imperatives* and *modal verbs*.

Imperatives	Modal verbs
warm up (line 22)	*should (line 32)*

FIGHTING FIT

Q I always see Boxers skipping when they're training for a bout – is it really that good a form of exercise? **AC, Solihull**

When it comes to exercise, boxers definitely know what's what. For burning fat, skipping is one of the best cardio exercises around.

A 75kg man can burn 850 calories an hour – a third more than running, and almost twice as much as cycling.

Because you're moving and supporting your whole bodyweight, you'll also raise your core body temperature much quicker. So if you're in a rush to get on to your main workout, warm up with a three-minute skip rather than doing a ten-minute run.

If it's technique you're worried about, follow these tips:

Choose your weapon: Select the right length of rope by standing on the middle and pulling the ends up – they should just reach your armpits.

Spot the ball: Land softly on the balls of your feet, not on your tiptoes. And only jump a couple of centimetres off the ground – if you can hear yourself land, you're jumping too high.

Go narrow: Keep your hands by your sides and your elbows tucked in, using only your wrists and forearms, and not your shoulders, to turn the rope. Keep looking straight ahead as peering down can strain your neck.

Kit up: Wear cross-trainers rather than running shoes, as they have more padding under the ball of the foot.

Once you've mastered the simple jump, you can try out different, more complicated jumps.

For more information contact the British Skipping Rope Association on 01527 854 194 (www.brsa.org.uk) or visit www.jumprope.com

Men's Health

Activity 3

Write a reply to this letter. Your reply should be between 100 and 150 words. Aim to:

- make helpful suggestions
- write in the present tense
- address your reader directly
- use imperatives and modal verbs.

I'm in Year 10 and trying to work hard at school but my parents are always fighting. My older sister says not to worry as they always argue, but I can't help it. It's making me fall behind with my school work. What should I do?

Worried, Manchester

Advice does not just come in the form of letters. Walk into any doctor's surgery or your school careers office and you will see plenty of advice sheets and leaflets on the tables and walls. Bookshops are full of the latest self-help books, offering advice on how to live your life. The following extract is taken from a traveller's handbook. It gives advice to inexperienced travellers.

When you write to advise you have to give a range of advice. Sometimes this is given directly and sometimes it is indirect. As you read the extract from *The Traveller's Handbook* on page 102, make a list, in note form, of the advice you are given.

Here are a few points to start with:

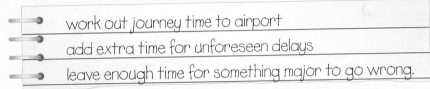

- work out journey time to airport
- add extra time for unforeseen delays
- leave enough time for something major to go wrong.

Variety of sentence structures

In order to make the subject more interesting, the writer uses a range of *sentence structures*:

Simple sentences, which communicate one idea, for example:

- This throws the driver a little. (line 16)
- A local dealer may be a police informer. (lines 28–29)

Compound sentences, which link two or more simple sentences with a conjunction such as *and*, *but*, and *or*, for example:

- A traveller's best friend is experience, and it can take dozens of trips to build this. (line 2)
- The Smiling Stranger has heard that one before and will offer to accompany you back to your hotel! (lines 23–24)

Complex sentences, which communicate more than one idea by using clauses, for example:

- Remember, too, to try and avoid travelling at peak periods such as Christmas, Easter and July and August, when families are taking their holidays. (lines 9–10)
- If you go prepared and adopt an understanding frame of mind, you should be able to manage without trouble. (lines 38–41)

Activity 5

Write a paragraph, offering a visitor to your area advice on shopping. You could include advice on where and when to go shopping and the best things to buy. Aim to include a range of *sentence structures* in your paragraph.

Staying Alive

Avoidable hassles

A traveller's best friend is experience, and it can take dozens of trips to build this. Fortunately, there are some tips that can be passed on to help the inexperienced traveller before they even step on a plane.

5 Travel planning

Most people have the good sense to work out their journey time to the airport and then add a little extra for unforeseen delays. But is that enough, should something major go wrong? What if the car breaks down or there are traffic tailbacks due to roadworks or an accident? Remember, too, to try and avoid travelling at peak periods
10 such as Christmas, Easter and July and August, when families are taking their holidays.

Taking taxis

What about the fare? Without a meter, the obvious foreigner will almost certainly be overcharged.

Two good tips for dealing with the drivers of unmetered taxis are:
15 **1** Know a little of the local language – at least enough to be able to say 'hello', 'please take me to …', 'how much?' and 'thank you'. This throws the driver a little.
2 Try and have the correct amount ready to hand over. It prevents the driver pleading that he has not got enough change.

Smiling strangers

20 Beware of the 'Smiling Stranger' when abroad. It is here that experience really counts, as it is often difficult to separate the con man from a genuinely friendly person. A favourite ploy is for him to offer his services as a guide. If he asks for cash, don't say 'I would like to help, but all my money is at the hotel'. The Smiling Stranger has heard that one before and will offer to accompany you back to your hotel!

25 The ultimate avoidable hassle

Do not try smuggling anything through customs, especially drugs. Soft drugs may be common in the countries you visit, but think twice before buying. A local dealer may be a police informer.
30 Prosecutions are becoming more common and penalties more severe – from ten years' hard labour to death.

The model visitor

There's no excuse for failing to research
35 the countries you intend to visit. Talk to people who have lived in or visited them and find out what problems you are likely to come across. If you go prepared and adopt an understanding
40 frame of mind, you should be able to manage without trouble.

from The Traveller's Handbook

Writing *your own*

An education magazine is running a competition for students:

Be the expert.
Advise your Head Teacher how to make your school a better place. Your writing should take the form of a leaflet to be pinned up in your Head's office.

Write your entry.
- **Your purpose is to advise on how to make your school a better place.**
- **Your audience is your Head Teacher and the judges of the competition.**

Follow these stages:

Stage 1

Choose three or four of the following. Make notes on the advice you want to give.

uniform	school rules	assemblies
length of lessons	punishments	rewards
subjects studied	careers advice	options
class groupings	teaching styles	things to do

Stage 2

- Decide on the best order for your advice. You might want to put the most important points first or last.
- Number your notes in the order in which you want to write about them.
- Think of sub-headings you could use to help organise your advice.

Stage 3

Read this example of how you could start your *advice leaflet*. The features of the writing are annotated for you:

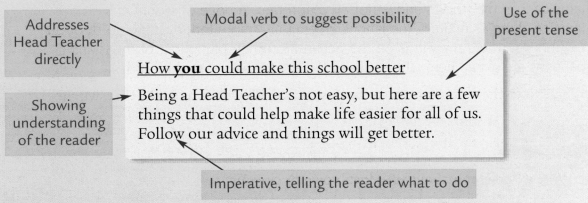

Addresses Head Teacher directly

Modal verb to suggest possibility

Use of the present tense

How **you** could make this school better

Being a Head Teacher's not easy, but here are a few things that could help make life easier for all of us. Follow our advice and things will get better.

Showing understanding of the reader

Imperative, telling the reader what to do

Now write your own advice leaflet. Remember to:
- address your reader directly
- show you understand your reader
- give clear advice
- write in the present tense
- use imperatives and modals
- use a variety of sentence structures.

5 Writing to inform

When you write to inform you are telling your reader about something or someone. The aim is to be interesting and to give new or original information. This kind of writing appears in:

- autobiographies
- biographies
- travel writing
- information leaflets
- newspaper and magazine articles .

Range of detail

This type of writing should always contain a range of detail that informs the reader. This may be a combination of *facts* and *opinions*.

Activity 1

Read the information text on the opposite page carefully.

As you read, answer the questions that surround the text. These help you to identify some of the features of writing to inform.

Present tense

Writing to inform is sometimes written in the *present tense*. The writer uses the present tense in this extract because this is the way Jamaica is now:

Jamaica is in the tropics and is hot all year round. A ridge of mountains divides Jamaica along its middle. The land is greener and more fertile to the north of the mountains, where the winds off the ocean drop their rain. Most of the island's bananas are grown here. The south of Jamaica is drier than the north.

Where does the writer switch to the past tense? Why does he make this switch?

Activity 2

Write a paragraph about your local town or city. Aim to:

- include a range of detail
- make the detail interesting for your reader
- write in the present tense.

Re-read your paragraph to check that it is clear, informative and interesting.

Jamaica

Jamaica is one of the islands in the Caribbean. Some people think it is shaped like a turtle, swimming between the USA and South America.

5 The island is 230 kilometres long, from west to east, and 80 kilometres at its widest point, from north to south. Jamaica covers an area of nearly 11,000 square kilometres, which is about half the size of Wales. About the same number of people live on one square

10 kilometre of land in Jamaica as on the same area in the United Kingdom. This means the two countries have the same population density.

Climate

Jamaica is in the tropics and is hot all year round. A ridge of

15 mountains divides Jamaica along its middle. The land is greener and more fertile to the north of the mountains, where the winds off the ocean drop their rain. Most of the island's bananas are grown here. The south of Jamaica is drier than the north. Sugar cane grows well here on flat land by the side of rivers. Jamaica lies in a hurricane

20 zone. In 1988 Hurricane Gilbert destroyed thousands of buildings and caused massive damage and flooding.

Montego Bay

Montego Bay is Jamaica's second-biggest city. It is on the northwest coast of the island. About 85,000 people live there. Montego Bay is a

25 busy port and many tourists arrive here first when they visit Jamaica. They come either by cruise ship from North America, or by aeroplane to Montego Bay's international airport. Flights arrive here from all over the world. It takes about nine hours to fly from London, and less than two hours from Florida, USA.

World Focus: Jamaica

Why do you think the writer tells you about this opinion?

Which countries is Jamaica linked to? Why do you think the writer makes these links?

What does this section tell you about:
● the climate
● the geography
● the crops?

Why do you think the writer uses sub-headings?

How many times has the writer used figures? Why do you think he uses figures?

Why do you think the writer gives details on how people get to Jamaica?

Personal writing

The last text you read was written in the *third person*, for example:

| it is | they are |

But writing to inform can often be more personal and written in the *first person*, for example:

| I am | we are |

Read the following text in which Smita Patel, a second-generation Indian, recalls her arrival at the city of Delhi with her boyfriend. As she is writing about things that have happened in the past, she uses the *past tense*.

Text B

I remember arriving at Delhi airport at 3 a.m., feeling apprehensive and excited. I was really no more knowledgeable about what to expect than any other Western traveller. It was now 6 a.m. and though the sun had barely risen we were shocked by the sheer volume of people. The whole area outside
5 the airport was packed with families, beggars, police, rickshaw wallahs, fruit vendors, taxi men, and of course the famed hotel sellers, relentlessly directing us to the 'best room in town'. Luckily we had met an American woman on the plane who was being met by her brother and despite being heavily jet-lagged we managed to struggle out of the chaos and find them. Ben had been living
10 on a low budget for a year and we were soon jostled towards India's cheapest mode of transport, the local bus. It looked ancient and I was convinced it would never manage the long ride into Delhi city.

Our first impressions were of sharp images of life glimpsed through the bus window. It took about an hour to reach the city. We travelled along a road
15 marked by small dwellings and shanty towns made out of paper, cardboard, rubber, tin, in fact anything that the poor could get their hands on. Even though I had witnessed such scenes as a child and heard of India's poverty, I was still bewildered at the extreme deprivation we were to come across during our stay.

'Between Two Cultures' by Smita Patel

Activity 3

As this writing is personal, it contains a number of personal experiences, feelings and opinions, for example:

- feeling apprehensive and excited
- I was really no more knowledgeable about what to expect than any other Western traveller.

Pick out and copy **at least four** more examples of the use of personal experiences, feelings or opinions from **Text B**.

Think of a place you have visited. Using the *past tense* and the *first person* (I, we), write one sentence about each of the following:

- your thoughts on the place before you got there
- how you felt when you arrived
- your feelings about the people who were there
- your thoughts on the place halfway through the visit
- how you felt when you left.

Range of sentence structures

Look back at **Texts A** and **B.** Both writers use a range of *sentence structures* to make their writing more interesting to read:

Simple sentences which communicate one idea, for example:

> **Text A:** Jamaica is one of the islands in the Caribbean. (line 1)
> **Text B:** It took about an hour to reach the city. (line 14)

Compound sentences, which link two or more simple sentences with a conjunction such as *and*, *but* and *or*, for example:

> **Text A:** Jamaica is in the tropics and is hot all year round. (line 14)
> **Text B:** Ben had been living on a low budget for a year and we were soon jostled towards India's cheapest mode of transport, the local bus. (lines 9–11)

Complex sentences, which communicate more than one idea by using *clauses*. The clauses are usually separated by a comma, for example:

> **Text A:** Jamaica covers an area of nearly 11,000 square kilometres, which is about half the size of Wales. (lines 7–9)
> **Text B:** Even though I had witnessed such scenes as a child and heard of India's poverty, I was still bewildered at the extreme deprivation we were to come across during our stay. (lines 16–19)

Here are two more examples of *complex sentences*:

- Even though I had eaten a large breakfast, I was still hungry.
- Even though the boy had read about London, he was still surprised by its size and the noise of the traffic.

Use this pattern to help you write **three** complex sentences of your own.

Writing *your own*

I am a student from New Zealand. My family are moving to England and I will be going to school there. I know very little about the country or the people. Could your readers write to me with any information they think might help me?

Yours with thanks,
John Simmons

You read the above letter in your favourite magazine and decide to reply.
Write a letter to John informing him about your home area and the people in it.

Your audience is John. Follow these stages:

Stage 1

Aim to write 3–4 clear and detailed paragraphs.

You have already written about your local town or city in Activity 2. You could use this for your first paragraph.

Your other paragraphs could be about:
- the people
- the climate
- what the schools are like.

Stage 2

Think about the personal details you could include. They might be to do with where you live and how long you've lived there, or particular things that have happened to you. Make a list of these.

Stage 3

You are now ready to start writing. When writing an *informal letter*, remember to organise your ideas into paragraphs, write in the present tense and make your letter interesting and informative. The structure of an informal letter is slightly different to the formal letter on page 97:

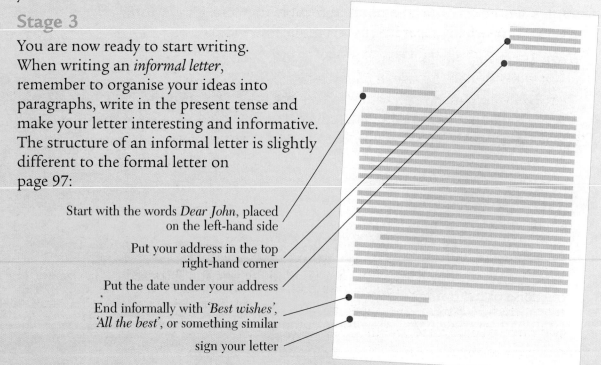

Start with the words *Dear John*, placed on the left-hand side

Put your address in the top right-hand corner

Put the date under your address

End informally with '*Best wishes*', '*All the best*', or something similar

sign your letter

6 Writing to explain

When you *write to explain*, your aim is to tell your reader *why* or *how* something has happened, is happening or will happen. You give the *reasons* for something.

The following texts show the same situation from two very different points of view. In the first text a mother explains:

- how she felt when her daughter was late home from school
- why she felt this way.

Activity 1

Read the text closely and answer the questions in the margin.

The mother

I began to worry and fidget by half past five. Two buses had gone by and she had not come home from school. I thought of all the places she could go to and became afraid because there were so many. My husband was working in Glasgow and my
5 father, who stayed with us, was on holiday. The house was empty. I was afraid. Not of being alone but she would have phoned to tell me if she was going away anywhere. My stomach turned, I felt hungry but could not eat, tired but could not sleep, tormented by my imagination.

10   At six o'clock I phoned her friend but she had no idea where she was and suggested I phone several people who were other schoolfriends. I phoned them all but no one knew and said they would phone back if they found out where she was. I took the car into town. There was a girl she was friendly with
15 who lived in a house on the way to town. She hadn't a phone so I went to the door.

‘Elaine, have you seen Cathie?’ It was hard to speak as the cries of pain echoed through my head. I was too embarrassed to stay, I had started to cry and my eyes were red and sore. I
20 went into all the cafés she talked of. It was no use. I went home and found myself waiting for the phone to ring. It did several times. Always someone to ask if I had found her. At nine o'clock I answered the phone for the millionth time. It was Mrs Wilson, Elaine's mother. She said Cathie was at their

What different reasons does the mother give to explain why she began to worry?

What did she do?

cont...

25　house. I felt as though the greatest load had been lifted from my heart. Again I took the car and drove into town. Cathie was very quiet and looked at me coldly. She thanked Elaine and got into the car. We said nothing but I wanted to be angry, I wanted to show how worried I had been. I knew that

30　she would not see my anger as love for her. It seemed as though she hated me and wanted to hurt me, but I could tell as she sat stiffly and unmoved that she had no idea that this was possible. I was as pleasant as I could be and she answered all the countless questions in a calm indifferent manner. I had

35　failed. I could not get through to her. She could not see the agony I had gone through because of her. It was my fault she was as she was. I had brought myself pain.

A Mother's Fondness by **Marion Rachel Stewart**

How did she feel when she got the phone call from Elaine's mother?

Why did she want to show her anger? Why did she decide not to?

Why did she feel she had failed?

Think about these two situations which show conflict between a parent and child:

Situation 1: The parent wants the child to tidy his/her bedroom. The child wants to go out.

Situation 2: The parent wants the child to stop seeing a particular friend. The child won't agree to this.

For each situation, list the reasons the parent might give to explain:
- *how* s/he feels
- *why* s/he feels this way.

In the next text it is the daughter's turn to explain what happened. The features of the explanation are annotated for you.

The daughter

After school I met Caroline and, as she had borrowed some records of mine, I decided to go round to her house and collect them. I didn't feel like going home anyway – perhaps it was because I was getting annoyed with my mother – well, not annoyed but it had
5 become too tense being with her. We couldn't have a conversation without it becoming a row. I think she resented me a bit. I don't know why. It made things easier when I went out; I didn't have to face up to her. She really annoyed me sometimes because any row was forgotten too quickly, as though it was a routine, as though
10 she wasn't bothered. She made me feel foolish and small. It was horrible, I hated it happening. I had begun to keep out of her way as much as possible.

Caroline and I had a good long talk about school and other things that worried us. We listened to records for ages in complete
15 silence, not saying a word. I suddenly realised I had missed both buses and would have to try and get the eight o'clock one.

Caroline decided we should go to the loch until it was time for my bus. By the time we had walked across the causeway and back I had missed it.
20 'Mum'll go daft,' I said suddenly, beginning to worry.
'Look, she's going to be mad anyway so it doesn't matter how late you are.'

'No, I'd better go now,' I said. I left and started walking through town. I was passing Elaine's house so I went in to see her.

Gives a number of reasons to explain why she didn't go home.

Explains how she came to miss the buses.

Uses direct speech to show how:
- she felt about being late
- she learnt about her mother's actions
- she felt about her mother's actions.

↓*cont…*

25   'Your mother's going daft, she's been phoning everyone. She was here, she was in town twice, she's even been to the police station.' Elaine stopped and took my arm.

    'Oh God,' I said, 'Oh no, you're joking!'

I sat down and buried my face in my hands. She would be

30 furious. What was I going to say to her? This meant another row.

    'Elaine, I don't want to go home. Can't I stay here?'

    'You'll have to face up to her as soon as possible. That's typical of you Cathie, run away from everything. You'll have to face up to it.'

35 Mrs Wilson came in. I was scared she would be angry too.

    'Cathie, I'm going to the phone box to phone your mother now.'

    My mother knocked on the door and Elaine answered. She stood quietly at the living room door.

I was angry. There had been so much fuss and now she was acting

40 as if nothing had happened. I thanked Elaine and got into the car. I didn't see any point in talking about it so I kept very quiet and pretended I wasn't bothered. She didn't even ask where I'd been until we were halfway home.

There was no way I could show her how hurt I really was. She

45 simply didn't care about me and I couldn't let her see how much that hurts. It was no good: she had already forgotten it – just like everything else.

> Explains why she felt angry and hurt.

A Mother's Fondness by **Marion Rachel Stewart**

Connectives

A *connective* is a word or phrase that can be used to:

- link parts of a sentence, for example:

  She hadn't a phone **so** I went to the door.

- link two sentences, for example:

  I knew that she would not see my anger as love. **It seemed as though** she hated me and wanted to hurt me.

In writing to explain, connectives are used to introduce real or possible reasons to answer the questions Why? or How?

Activity 3

Read these sentences taken from the two texts. For each one, pick out and write down the *connectives* that answer the questions Why? or How?

1 I thought of all the places she could go to and became afraid because there were so many.

2 It was hard to speak as the cries of pain echoed through my head.

3 We said nothing but I wanted to be angry.

4 I didn't feel like going home anyway – perhaps it was because I was getting annoyed with my mother.

5 She really annoyed me sometimes because any row was forgotten too quickly.

6 I was passing Elaine's house so I went in to see her.

7 I didn't see any point in talking about it so I kept very quiet and pretended I wasn't bothered.

Activity 4

Think about both texts. Imagine you have been called in to help the mother and daughter sort out their differences. Explain:

Either the mother's point of view to the daughter

Or the daughter's point of view to the mother.

Remember you need to:

- focus on how they feel and why they feel this way
- use connectives to link ideas within sentences and between sentences.

Organising an explanation

When writing an explanation it is important to organise your ideas clearly in a logical order. One way of doing this is to use a *chronological order*, which is the order in which things happen.

I don't remember having any problems at primary school. The trouble really started when I went to secondary. I was used to a small school where everybody knew everybody else – if anything went wrong my Mam always got to know and it was sorted pretty quickly. When I went to secondary it was different. Most of my friends had gone to other schools and I had to start making friends quickly. Looking back, I guess the friends I made just weren't into school work and some of them enjoyed making life difficult for the teachers.

My reports in Years 7 and 8 were OK. Some of the teachers said I could do better but most of them said I was making satisfactory progress. By Year 9 it was a different story. I'd given up on work altogether and was desperate to impress my friends. Before I knew where I was, I was being sent out of class, put on report and given endless detentions. My report at the end of that year was a disaster! My parents went up to the school and when they got home my Dad was blazing and my Mam wouldn't even talk to me.

After that life got pretty bad. They tried to make me stay in and do my homework and I did everything I could to avoid it. Most of the time I'd get in from school, grab some tea and then clear off before they got back from work. There was usually a shouting match when I got home but there wasn't really anything they could do. Sometimes, just to keep the peace, I'd pretend to do some work but I'd always end up listening to music.

It wasn't until Year 11 that things started to settle a bit. I knew I had big exams coming up and that I had to start doing some work for them but by that time I was way behind with my assignments and didn't have a clue how to catch up. Then I met my girlfriend Cathy. She's really helped and sometimes I do my work round at her place. Things are better with Mam and Dad now as well. At least they've given up moaning at me. I know I've blown getting really good results but I'm hoping they'll be good enough to get me on the engineering course I want to do when I finish school. If I get that far, I'll count myself lucky.

Chris, North London

Read the text on the opposite page. In the first paragraph, the writer explains why there were no problems in primary school and why he had to make friends quickly in secondary school.

Write **three sentences** to sum up what the writer explains in the second, third and fourth paragraphs, starting like this:

In the second (third, fourth) paragraph he explains ...

The writer chose to write his explanation in the order in which things happened. He could have chosen a different way:

- He could have started by describing the present situation and then explained how it happened.

> I'm just two weeks away from my GCSEs and working hard. It hasn't always been that way though. I've spent much of the last two years wasting time and trying to avoid anything that might require a bit of effort. My problems all started when ...

- He could have started in the middle:

> Year 9 was almost certainly my worst year at school. I was desperate to impress my friends and had given up on work altogether. I was always being sent out of class or put on report and I had endless detentions. My report at the end of that year was a disaster!
>   It hadn't always been like that though ...

When writing an explanation you can choose where to start.

Writing *your own*

Choose something that has happened that has had a strong effect on you. Explain:
- **what happened**
- **why and how it happened**
- **how you felt about it**
- **why it had a strong effect on you.**

Follow these stages:

Stage 1

Decide what you are going to write about. Here are some suggestions:

- meeting someone new
- a mistake you made
- winning a competition or match
- an accident.

Stage 2

Once you have made your choice, use the bullet points in the question to help you gather ideas.

Stage 3

Compare these two plans for writing about winning a competition:

Plan 1

<u>what happened</u>: won swimming competition
<u>why and how it happened</u>: best one there – won by 5 metres
<u>how you felt about it</u>: really happy
<u>why it was so important</u>: because I'd always wanted to win it

There is not enough detail in this plan to help you write your explanation.

Plan 2

<u>what happened</u>: won swimming competition – 6 months ago – county swimming championships – entered for 200 metres crawl – spent all morning watching other races – really nervous – friends were there – and family – all cheering me on

<u>why and how it happened</u>: a lot of training (give details) – selected for county after winning other competitions – my coach – other swimmers in the race – whistle blew – good dive – neck and neck at halfway – felt really strong – thought of all the hard work – concentrated on finishing – realised I'd won

<u>how you felt about it</u>: really happy – excited – jumped out of pool – hugged friends – proud when receiving medal – went out to celebrate

<u>why it was so important</u>: always wanted to win – worked hard – other people's efforts – sense of achievement – proved I could do it

A plan like this will help you to explain clearly and in detail.

Now plan your own ideas, using Plan 2 as a model.

Stage 4

Once your plan is complete, you are ready to start writing. Remember to answer the questions Why? and How?

7 Writing to describe

When you *write to describe,* you are trying to paint a picture with words. Your aim is to make the place or the people or the thing you are describing seem real to the reader.

Detail

It is important to give *detail* so that the reader can form a picture of what is being described.

Brian Keenan was a lecturer in a university in Beirut. He was kidnapped one morning on his way to work. It was four and a half years before he was released. In the following passage he describes his prison cell.

I had, of course, like all of us, seen prison cells. We have all seen films about prisoners, or read books about prison life. Some of the great stories of escape and imprisonment are part of our history. It seems much of our culture is laden with these stories. But when I think back to that cell, I know that
5 nothing that I had seen before could compare with that most dismal of places. I will describe it briefly to you, that you may see it for yourself.
  It was built very shoddily of rough-cut concrete blocks haphazardly put together and joined by crude slapdash cement-work. Inside, and only on the inside, the walls were plastered over with that same dull grey cement.
10 There was no paint. There was no colour, just the constant monotony of rough grey concrete. The cell was six feet long and four feet wide. I could stand up and touch those walls with my outstretched hands and walk those six feet in no more than four paces. On the floor was a foam mattress. With the mattress laid out I had a pacing stage of little more than
15 a foot's width.
  In one corner there was a bottle of water which I replenished daily when I went to the toilet, and in another corner was a bottle for urine, which I took with me to empty. There was also a plastic cup in which I kept a much abused and broken toothbrush. On the mattress was an old, ragged,
20 filthy cover. It had originally been a curtain. There was one blanket which I never used, due to the heat, the filth and the heavy smell, stale and almost putrid, of the last person who had slept here. The cell had no windows. A sheet steel door was padlocked every day, sounding like a thump on the head to remind me where I was. At the head of the mattress
25 I kept my briefcase with my school text books. Behind the briefcase I hid my shoes. I was forever afraid that I would lose those shoes. If I did, I felt it would be a sure sign that I would never leave that cell.

An Evil Cradling by **Brian Keenan**

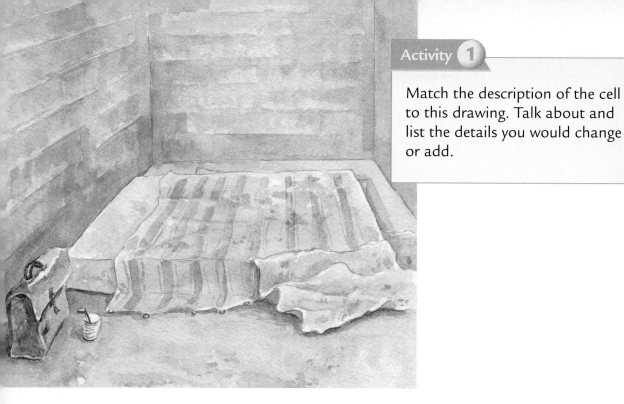

Activity 1

Match the description of the cell to this drawing. Talk about and list the details you would change or add.

Adjectives

It is not just the detail that is important in a description. Words that are chosen to describe things help the reader to build up a picture. These words are called *adjectives*. What do the following adjectives tell you about the things they are describing?

- <u>crude slapdash</u> cement-work
- <u>rough grey</u> concrete
- a <u>much abused</u> and <u>broken</u> toothbrush
- an <u>old</u>, <u>ragged</u>, <u>filthy</u> cover
- the <u>heavy</u> smell, <u>stale</u> and almost <u>putrid</u>

Now think about these together. What impression do they create of this place?

Activity 2

1 Look around your classroom. List five things in the classroom, for example: desks.

2 Think about what your classroom is like. Is it:
   - bright and cheerful
   - dull and depressing
   - new and shiny
   - old and tatty?

3 For each detail you listed in question 1, choose at least two appropriate *adjectives* and underline them. Your adjectives should describe the thing **and** help to describe what the classroom is like.
   For example:

   bright and cheerful   *old and tatty*
              ↓   ↓
   <u>glossy</u>, <u>varnished</u> desks   <u>scratched</u>, <u>dingy</u> desks

Organisation

A good description contains *well-organised ideas*. Notice how in Brian Keenan's description, one idea often leads into another:

> At the head of the mattress I kept my briefcase with my school text books. Behind the briefcase I hid my shoes. I was forever afraid that I would lose those shoes. If I did, I felt it would be a sure sign that I would never leave that cell.

The colours show you the links between the ideas in the sentences. Keenan links the briefcase to the shoes to his fear of losing the shoes and the reason for this fear.

Activity 3

1. Copy and complete the following sentences.
2. Then write two more sentences which continue the same ideas. Use the sentences above as a model.

At the foot of my bed I kept my school bag with my books. Behind the

bag I hid my _____ .

Similes

Writers often use *similes* to describe. A simile is when one thing is compared to another to paint a clearer picture. Read the following text closely and answer the questions about the writer's use of similes:

What is his face compared to? What does this comparison suggest about his face?

How would you expect someone wearing thick leather boots to move? What is unexpected about the way Donald MacFarlane moves?

Think about the whole description. What kind of person do you think Donald MacFarlane is?

> Donald MacFarlane, the snake-man, may have been old and small but he was an impressive looking character. His eyes were pale blue, deep-set in a face round and dark and wrinkled as a walnut. Above the blue eyes, the eyebrows were thick and startlingly white but the hair on his head was almost black. In spite of the thick leather boots, he moved like a leopard, with soft low cat-like strides.

Going Solo by **Roald Dahl**

Write four sentences describing someone you know well. Use the description of Donald MacFarlane as a model for your writing.

- In your first sentence, name the person and say something about his or her appearance.
- In the second sentence, describe the eyes and use a *simile* to describe the face.
- In the third sentence, describe the eyebrows and hair.
- In the fourth sentence, use a simile to describe the way s/he moves.

Atmosphere and mood

As you have seen, descriptions often do more than tell you about a place or a person. They can give you an idea of what it feels like to be in that place or with that person; they can create an *atmosphere* or *mood*. They sometimes do this by using some or all of the five senses: sight, hearing, taste, smell and touch.

Activity 5

Read the following text closely.

1 Where does the writer use the following two senses to help create atmosphere:
- smell
- hearing?

2 Talk about:
- what this place feels like to you
- places you know that are similar to it
- whether you would like to go to a place like this.

I could not keep away from Gala Land. It had a particular smell which drew me down the steep flight of concrete steps to the pay desk below. It was built underground in a sort of valley between two outcrops of rock, over which was a ribbed glass roof. The walls were covered in
5   greenish moss and the whole place had a close, damp, musty smell and, although it was lit from end to end with neon lights, everything looked somehow dark, furtive and gone to seed. Some of the booths were closed down and those which kept open must have lost money, except perhaps on the few days when parties of trippers came from
10   inland, in the teeth of the weather, and dived for shelter to the underground fun palace. Then, for a few hours, the fruit and try-your-strength and fortune card machines whirred, loud cracks echoed from the rifle ranges and hurdygurdy music sounded. For the rest of the time the place contained a few unemployed men and teenager boys, who
15   chewed gum and fired endless rounds of blank ammunition at the bobbing rows of duck targets.

from *A Bit of Singing and Dancing* by Susan Hill

Contrast

In the last two sentences the writer shows 'Gala Land' in different ways; she presents a *contrast*:

When it is busy	When it is not busy
Then, for a few hours, the fruit and try-your-strength and fortune card machines whirred, loud cracks echoed from the rifle ranges and hurdygurdy music sounded.	For the rest of the time the place contained a few unemployed men and teenager boys, who chewed gum and fired endless rounds of blank ammunition at the bobbing rows of duck targets.

What different atmospheres are created in these sentences?

When writing to describe, it is often helpful to present a contrast by writing about a place at different times.

Activity 6

Choose one of the following places:
- a shopping centre
- a park
- a cemetery.

Now write:
- a paragraph describing it in the day
- a paragraph describing it at night.

Aim to create two different atmospheres in your descriptions. Your paragraphs should each contain about six sentences.

Writing *your own*

Describe a room you know well. It could be your bedroom, a classroom or somewhere else. Aim to make your description interesting for your reader.

Follow these stages:

Stage 1

Picture the room in your mind. Make a list of details about:
- the size and shape of the room
- the colours in the room
- the furniture in the room.

Think of adjectives that help to describe these more clearly, for example, a *large, rectangular* shape, a *jet black* carpet, an *old* and *worn* desk.

Stage 2

Think about the people who spend time in the room. What personal possessions are there? For example: books, magazines, posters, photographs.
Think of similes to describe some of these, for example:
Magazines lie scattered on the floor *like* empty sweet wrappers.

Stage 3

What does the room feel like? Which of these words best suit the way it feels?

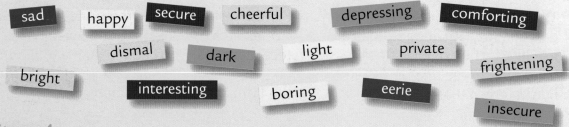

sad   happy   secure   cheerful   depressing   comforting
dismal   dark   light   private
bright   interesting   boring   eerie   frightening   insecure

Stage 4

Are you going to be in the room, describing what you see from the inside? Or are you going to be looking in at it from the outside? Here are some suggestions for an opening sentence:
- I peered through the dirty window pane to see a small and very untidy bedroom.
- I lay on my bed and silently studied my bedroom.
- Having opened the door into the empty room, I stepped through.

Stage 5

Now write your description. Remember your aim is to paint a picture of the room for your reader.

SECTION C EXAM PRACTICE

Paper 1

This paper examines **Reading** in Section A and **Writing** in Section B. Each section is worth 15% of your final mark in English.

Section A requires reading responses to non-fiction and media texts. There will be two or more texts. You need to show that you:
- understand what the texts are about
- can tell the difference between fact and opinion
- can follow an argument
- can write about how material is presented
- can select the right information to answer the questions.

Section B requires writing which argues, persuades or advises. This may be linked to the materials in Section A. You will be given a choice of questions and need to show that you can:
- communicate your ideas clearly
- write for purpose and audience
- organise your ideas into sentences and paragraphs
- use a range of words
- use a range of sentence structures
- spell and punctuate accurately.

Practice Paper 1

Section A: Reading

Answer **all** the questions in this section.
Spend about **60 minutes** on this section.

Read the media text, **Who cares what goes down the drain?**, and the non-fiction text, **Pollution**.

1 **Who cares what goes down the drain?** is a media text. What have you found out about:
   - its intended purpose
   - its intended audience
   - how the picture is used to get the meaning across? (6 marks)

2 **a** What opinion does the writer express in lines 13 to 14 of **Pollution**? (2 marks)
   b List **two facts** and **two opinions** which are used in the rest of the text to support this opinion. (4 marks)

3 Re-read lines 1 to 8 of **Pollution**.
   a List **two** examples of the writer using language to persuade the reader. (2 marks)
   b For **each** example, explain **how** the writer is using language to persuade. (4 marks)

4 Think about **both** texts and the arguments they present. **Compare**:
   - what each text shows you about what is happening to the earth
   - what each text shows you about why this is happening
   - how well you think each text works. (9 marks)

(Total: 27 marks)

WHO CARES WHAT GOES
DOWN THE DRAIN?

80% of marine pollution comes from the land – from industry, from agriculture, and from our homes. Pollution weakens marine mammals' immunity to disease, and may be a factor in the recent rise in recorded deaths of dolphins, whales and porpoises.
That's why WWF is sponsoring research into the effects of pollution in these mammals, and lobbying for a Marine Act to protect our seas. Our immune systems are similar to those of marine mammals.
One more reason not to leave polluted seas to the next generation.
To find out what you can do to help, call 01483 426 333 or visit www.wwf.org.uk/whocares

TAKING ACTION FOR A LIVING PLANET

WWF

Pollution

Over the last fifty years, pollution has become one of the most serious problems facing society. Pollution kills. It chokes rivers, smothers life in the oceans, poisons the air and despoils the land. Pollution is the presence in the environment of large quantities of dangerous chemicals, many created by people, that can harm life and
5 cause long-lasting damage to our planet. Pollution can be obvious, like an oil slick on the surface of the sea, or less obvious, like chemicals sprayed onto fields to kill pests. Pollution is the price the world is paying for rapid agricultural and industrial development – without consideration of its effects on the environment.

Pollution is often the consequence of ignorance, carelessness or attempts to
10 save money when releasing a chemical into the environment. It is not, however, just factories, power stations and farmers who create pollution. We are all responsible, whether driving a car or dropping litter in the street.

Pollution must be controlled, because if the problem is not resolved, then every living thing on this planet could disappear. No organism, no matter how large or
15 how small, can escape the poisonous chemicals of pollution. Pollution has already brought some species of wildlife to the brink of extinction.

Fish all over the world are vulnerable to pollution. A dramatic example occurred after a fire at a chemical plant in Switzerland in November 1986. As a result of the fire, extremely poisonous chemicals were washed into the Rhine River in
20 Europe. Over half a million fish, including 150,000 eels, were wiped out. All life in a 320-kilometre (200-mile) stretch of the river was killed.

Section B: Writing to argue, persuade or advise

Either

5 Write an article for a magazine in which you **argue** that people should do more to fight pollution. Aim to:
- make your key points clearly
- support your argument with evidence and examples
- choose the right language for a magazine article.   (27 marks)

Or

6 Your year group has decided to have a sponsored run to raise money for a charity. Decide what the charity is and write a letter to parents **persuading** them to sponsor students in support of this charity. Aim to:
- give reasons why they should support this charity
- use language to persuade
- choose the right language for a letter to parents.   (27 marks)

Or

7 Charities sometimes find it difficult to get teenagers interested in raising money. Write a leaflet for charities in which you **advise** them how to get teenagers to help. Aim to:
- make suggestions about how they could involve teenagers
- advise them on the types of things that might interest teenagers
- choose the right language for an advice leaflet.   (27 marks)

Or

8 What would you do to make the world a better place? Write an article for a national newspaper in which you **argue** your point of view and try to **persuade** readers to agree with you. Aim to:
- make your key points clearly
- use language to argue and persuade
- choose the right language for a newspaper article.   (27 marks)

The examiner comments ...
Section A

There are two texts. One is non-fiction and one is media.
Questions **1** to **4** target the Assessment Objectives.

QUESTION 1 asks you to show you can:
- identify the writer's purpose and audience
- evaluate how information is presented.

Answer these questions in order to write about:
- **Purpose**: What different things is the poster trying to achieve? Why do you think this?

- **Audience**: Who is it trying to influence? Why do you think this?

- **The picture**: What are your first impressions? What is the background detail? What is in the foreground? What do the expressions on the children's faces tell you about what they are thinking? What T-shirt is the boy wearing? How does this help you to understand what he might be thinking? Why do you think the dolphin is dead? What makes you think this?

QUESTION 2 asks you to show you can:
- tell the difference between fact and opinion
- select material appropriate to purpose.

a Read these lines referred to in the question:

> 'Pollution must be controlled, because if the problem is not resolved, then every living thing on this planet could disappear.'

Using your own words, explain what the writer is saying. Start with:
'He thinks that ...'

b The easiest place to find facts is where there are figures. Look at the information box. Choose two facts from this and copy them.

c Opinions cannot be proved to be true. They are sometimes stated as facts. Find and copy two opinions from the text.

QUESTION 3 asks you to show you can:
- understand how the writer uses language
- evaluate how the writer uses language.

Re-read the lines below, as instructed in the question. The annotations point out some of the features of the language. You need to copy two separate examples. For each example explain how the writer is using language to persuade.

Lists four separate things to show how much damage is being done. The verbs used (chokes, smothers, poisons and despoils) emphasise the danger.

Short sentence for emphasis.

> Over the last fifty years, pollution has become one of the most serious problems facing society. Pollution kills. It chokes rivers, smothers life in the oceans, poisons the air and despoils the land. Pollution is the presence in the environment of large quantities of dangerous chemicals, many created by people, that can harm life and cause long-lasting damage to our planet. Pollution can be obvious, like an oil slick on the surface of the sea, or less obvious, like chemicals sprayed onto fields to kill pests. Pollution is the price the world is paying for rapid agricultural and industrial development – without consideration of its effects on the environment.

Starts four sentences with the word 'pollution' to emphasise that there is a lot of it about.

QUESTION 4 asks you to show you can:
- follow an argument
- evaluate an argument
- make cross references and use material from different texts.

There are three marks for each bullet point in the question so you must deal with each one.

To answer the first one, sum up the key points made about pollution in both texts. Remember, points can be made through pictures as well as through words.

To answer the second, identify the causes of the pollution given in both texts.

To answer the third, clearly state what you think about each text. Give as many reasons as you can for why you think this.

Section B

Follow these steps:

Step 1

Spend a few minutes thinking about each task. Choose the one you can do best. Make sure you know:

- **who** you are writing for
- **why** you are writing
- **what** you are writing
- **the kind** of writing you need to do.

For example:

5 Write an article for a magazine in which you **argue** that people should do more to fight pollution.

What: you are writing an article

Who: you are writing for the readers of the magazine

The kind: writing to argue

Why: to argue that people should do more

Aim to:

- make your key points clearly
- support your argument with evidence and examples
- choose the right language for a magazine article.

Step 2

Gather ideas connected to what you are writing, for example:

pollution kills · harm to wildlife · chemicals · litter · join WWF · must act now · use bottle banks · **ARGUE: people should do more to fight pollution** · too many cars · walk short journeys · what we can do? · asthma · air pollution

Step 3

Decide on an order for your ideas. You could number them.
Think about the kind of language you should use, for example:

- **rhetorical questions**: are you prepared to watch your planet die?
- **emotive language**: the senseless destruction of innocent animals.

Think about how you should organise your article.
You could use sub-headings. You **must** use paragraphs.

Step 4

Stop and read what you have written after each paragraph. Research shows this helps students to produce better writing.
When you have finished:

- read through carefully to check it makes clear sense
- add or cross out words
- correct any mistakes in spelling and punctuation.

Paper 2

This paper examines **Reading** in Section A and **Writing** in Section B. Each section is worth 15% of your final mark in English.

Section A requires a reading response to poetry from different cultures and traditions. This poetry is in Section 1 of the **AQA Anthology**. You need to show that you:
- understand what the poems are about
- can select the right information to answer the questions
- can write about the ways poets present their ideas
- can make appropriate reference to the poems.

Section B requires writing which informs, explains or describes. Some of the tasks may be linked to themes in the poems. You will be given a choice of questions and need to show that you can:
- communicate your ideas clearly
- write for purpose and audience
- organise your ideas into sentences and paragraphs
- use a range of words
- use a range of sentence structures
- spell and punctuate accurately.

Practice Paper 2

Section A: Reading

This section relates to Section 1 of the 2004 **AQA Anthology** that you have been using during the course.

Answer **one** question from this section on the poems you have studied in Section 1 of the Anthology: Different Cultures.
Spend about **45 minutes** on this section.

Either

1 Compare how the poets show you something important about the culture or cultures they are writing about in **Blessing** and **one** other poem.
   Write about:
   • what you are shown about the culture(s)
   • how the language brings out what the culture(s) are like
   • what the poets seem to think about the culture(s)
   • what you think about the culture(s).   (27 marks)

Or

2 Compare what you are shown about conflict between cultures in **Presents from my Aunts in Pakistan** with what you are shown about conflict between cultures in **one** other poem.
   Write about:
   • what you are shown about conflict between cultures
   • how the poets use language to show this conflict
   • how the poets seem to feel about this conflict
   • your opinion on what you are shown.   (27 marks)

Section B: Writing to inform, explain or describe

Answer **one** question in this section.
Spend about **45 minutes** on this section.

REMEMBER:
- Spend about 5 minutes planning and sequencing your material
- Try to write at least 1½ sides
- Spend about 5 minutes checking
  - ✔ your paragraphing
  - ✔ your punctuation
  - ✔ your spelling.

Either

3 Many people have interests to which they give a great deal of time, effort and money. Write **informatively** about an interest of yours. Make clear:
- what the interest is
- what the interest involves
- the ways in which the interest is important to you. (27 marks)

Or

4 Lottery winners sometimes say the money has not made them happy. Imagine you have won one million pounds on the lottery. **Explain** how you would spend the money and why you would spend it in this way. (27 marks)

Or

5 **Describe** a person you know well. Aim to make your description lively and interesting. (27 marks)

Or

6 Many people have family traditions. These may be to do with how they celebrate holidays or religious festivals. **Describe** a family tradition that is important to you and **explain** why it is important. (27 marks)

The examiner comments ...
Section A

Working with your Anthology
When you start to study the poems in your **Anthology** you need to think about:
- meaning
- presentation
- language.

Thinking about meaning
- Ask yourself questions about the meaning of the poems: Who? What? Where? When? Why? How?
- Are there other meanings buried beneath the surface?
- Is there a particular viewpoint developed in the poem?
- Does the poem tell you something about another culture?

Thinking about presentation
- How are the words set out on the page?
- Is there any repetition? What is the effect of this?
- Is rhyme used? Where? How does it affect the way the poem is read aloud?
- Is the rhythm regular or irregular? What effect does it have?

Thinking about language
- How does the poet use words to get across a particular idea?
- Are there any examples of specific techniques, such as similes?
- Is there anything unusual about the way the poet uses words?

Developing your own point of view
- When you know the poems well you are ready to start comparing them.
- Make lists of differences and similarities between them.
- Decide which poems you like most and least – be prepared to give your reasons.
- Brainstorm the things you have learnt about different cultures – which poem would you most like to have written? Why?

Writing about the poems in the examination

Read the questions carefully. Before making your choice, make sure:
- you have studied the named poem
- you can think of another suitable poem to write about.

Follow these steps:

Step 1

Highlight key words in the question, for example:
Compare how the poets show you something important about the culture or cultures they are writing about in **Blessing** and **one** other poem.
Write about:
- **what** you are shown about the culture(s)
- **how** the language brings out what the culture(s) are like
- **what** the poets seem to think about the culture(s)
- **what** you think about the culture(s).

Step 2

Brainstorm your ideas on the named poem and the poem of your choice, for example:

Try to include some useful quotations in your brainstorm.

Step 3

Aim to write about the poems in an organised way. Use the structure on page 76 to help you.

Section B

This section targets the same Assessment Objectives as Paper 1 Section B, but these questions tend to draw on personal experience. The writing is of a more personal kind than in Paper 1. There is less emphasis on a particular audience, though you should always be aware you are writing for an examiner.

Follow these steps:

Step 1

Spend a few minutes thinking about each task. Choose the one you can do best. Highlight key words in the question. For example:

6 Many people have family traditions. These may be to do with how they celebrate holidays or religious festivals. **Describe** a family tradition that is important to you and **explain** why it is important.

Step 2

Gather ideas connected to what you are writing, for example:

preparing all day   food/drink   chance for all the family to meet

DESCRIBE   how the house looks   **Family tradition: Christmas Eve party**   exchange presents   EXPLAIN

who comes   no more work to do

Step 3

Decide on an order for your ideas. You could number them.

Think about the kind of language you should use, for example:

Descriptive language: The <u>tinsel-covered</u> tree <u>glitters and shines</u> in the corner of the <u>candle-lit</u> room.

Connectives: One of the reasons it's so important to me is <u>because</u> all the family are there.

Remember you **must** organise your ideas into paragraphs.

Step 4

Stop and read what you have written after each paragraph. Research shows this helps to produce better writing.

When you have finished:

- read through carefully to check it makes clear sense
- add or cross out words
- correct any mistakes in spelling and punctuation.

Sample Paper 1

Section A: Reading

> Answer **all** the questions in this section.
> Spend about **60 minutes** on this section.

Read the media text, **New York**, and the non-fiction text, **Crime, punishment and zero tolerance**.

1 **New York** is a media text. What have you found out about:
   - its intended purpose
   - its intended audience
   - the pictures and how they are used to get across meaning. (6 marks)

2 **a** Why, according to the writer of **Crime, punishment and zero tolerance**, have the crime levels in New York dropped? (4 marks)
   b List **two facts** which he uses to support his argument. (2 marks)

3 Re-read these lines from **New York**:

> Make a vague plan of what you want to see, but beware – the fizzing energy of Manhattan is bewitching, and it could carry you completely off course. Never mind – adventures are always guaranteed in this amazing international metropolis. Just make sure you see the best sights, like the Empire State with its amazing views, and leave plenty of time for the fabulous shopping!

How does the writer use language to persuade the reader? Write about at least three words or phrases that persuade. (6 marks)

4 Think about **both** texts. **Compare**:
   - what each text shows you about New York
   - how the ideas are presented in each text
   - how well you think each text works. (9 marks)

(Total: 27 marks)

new york

★★★★★

star attractions
- World Class Dining, Drinking and Nightlife • Amazing Shopping • Empire State Building • Harbour Cruises
- Central Park Romance • Museum of Modern Art (MoMA) • Statue of Liberty • Chinatown • Greenwich Village
- Broadway Shows • Times Square

New York City isn't one place. It's a hundred different places, all jostling for your attention. From the uptown glitz of the Upper West Side to the downtown chic of the West Village, you are presented with entirely different sights, sounds and even smells in each neighbourhood. As if this weren't enough, interesting new areas keep springing up with their trendy acronyms. The latest is DUMBO (we kid you not – it stands for Down Under the Manhattan Bridge Overpass!).

Make a vague plan of what you want to see, but beware – the fizzing energy of Manhattan is bewitching, and it could carry you completely off course. Never mind – adventures are always guaranteed in this amazing international metropolis. Just make sure you see the best sights like the Empire State with its amazing views, and leave plenty of time for the fabulous shopping!

Crime, punishment and zero tolerance

*Read this carefully in case you don't believe it – **New York is one of America's safest cities**. The FBI keeps league tables of violent crimes and New York does not even make the first 100 places. Since 1990, the murder rate has dropped by more than 60 per cent. More significantly for tourists, 80 per cent of murder victims are known to their killers.*

Rudolph Giuliani, the Mayor from 1993 till 2001, has claimed much of the credit for the drop in crime. But a greater influence is probably William Bratton, the police commissioner forced out of office by Giuliani in 1996. It was Bratton who developed the 'broken window' theory of crime prevention. This has influenced police forces across America and Europe. He argued that by allowing estates to become run down, and failing to stop vandalism, litter and graffiti, you contributed to the creation of no-go areas. These would become hotbeds for more serious crime. Instead, by adopting 'zero tolerance' of crimes such as begging, drunkenness, drugs and prostitution, you encouraged an atmosphere in which the streets and subways felt safe. And as most crimes are committed by the same people, by arresting someone for jumping the turnstiles you may also catch a drug dealer with a handgun.

The results of this policy can be seen in the huge number of police on the streets – some 40,000 in all. The police may sometimes be heavy-handed but most people feel reassured by their presence. Streets and parks which were once no-go areas are now safe to walk about by day.

Section B: Writing to argue, persuade or advise

Answer **one** question in this section.
Spend about **45 minutes** on this section.

You may use some of the information from Section A if you want to, but you do not have to do so.

If you use any of the information, do not simply copy it.

REMEMBER:
- Spend about 5 minutes planning and sequencing your material
- Try to write at least 1½ sides
- Spend about 5 minutes checking
  - ✔ your paragraphing   ✔ your punctuation   ✔ your spelling.

Either

5 Write an article for a newspaper in which you **argue** that more could be done to fight crime in your area. Aim to:
- make your key points clearly
- support your argument with evidence and examples
- choose the right language for a newspaper article.   (27 marks)

Or

6 Write a leaflet, for use in a Tourist Information Office, advertising a place you know well. Your aim is to **persuade** people to want to go there. Aim to:
- give reasons why they should go there
- use language to persuade
- choose the right form for a leaflet but do not spend time on drawings.
                                                              (27 marks)

Or

7 Crime amongst teenagers is rising. Write an advice sheet **advising** teenagers on how to avoid crime **and** how to help friends who are involved in crime. Aim to:
- make suggestions on how to avoid crime
- make suggestions on how to help friends involved in crime
- choose the right language for an advice sheet for teenagers.   (27 marks)

Or

8 You have just returned from holiday and was disappointed with the place. It was not like the brochure showed it to be. Write a letter of complaint to the company to **advise** them on the changes they need to make to the brochure and to **persuade** them to give you your money back. Aim to:
- make your key points clearly
- choose language to advise and persuade
- choose the right language for a letter of complaint.   (27 marks)

Sample Paper 2

Section A: Reading

Answer one question from this section on the poems you have studied in
Section 1 of the **Anthology**: Different Cultures.
Spend about **45 minutes** on this section.

Either

1 Compare the way the poet organises the ideas in **What Were They Like?** with the
way the ideas are organised in **one** other poem.
Write about:

- what the ideas are

- how the ideas are organised in each poem

- similarities and differences in the ways the ideas are organised

- your opinion on the ways the ideas are organised.   (27 marks)

Or

2 Compare what you are shown about the importance of identity in **Search For My
Tongue** and **one** other poem.
Write about:

- what you are shown about the importance of identity in both poems

- how the poets show you these things

- what the poets seem to think about the importance of identity

- what you think about the poems.   (27 marks)

Section B: Writing to inform, explain or describe

Answer **one** question in this section.
Spend about **45 minutes** on this section.

REMEMBER:
- Spend about 5 minutes planning and sequencing your material
- Try to write at least 1½ sides
- Spend about 5 minutes checking
  - ✔ your paragraphing   ✔ your punctuation   ✔ your spelling.

Either

3 Write about a recent holiday you have had. **Inform** your reader of both the good and bad things about it.   (27 marks)

Or

4 Choose a person or a subject about which your feelings have changed. Write about what you used to think and feel, what you think and feel now and **explain** how the change has come about.   (27 marks)

Or

5 Choose one of the following places. **Describe** it at two different times of the year:
- a beach
- a town centre
- a park.   (27 marks)

Or

6 What would you like to be doing in five years' time? **Inform** the reader of your hopes for the future and **explain** how you intend to make them come true.
                                                          (27 marks)

Acknowledgements

The publishers gratefully acknowledge the following for permission to reproduce copyright material. Every effort has been made to contact copyright holders of material reproduced in this book. Any omissions will be rectified in subsequent printings if notice is given to the publishers.

p5 Beehive Communications for the cover of a Eurolines leaflet; p9 The *Northern Echo* for 'Nightmare fate of a dream machine' by Nigel Burton, 31st December 1997; p11 The *Guardian* for 'review of Blade II' by Phelim O'Neill, from 'The Guide', the *Guardian*, 28th September 2002 © The *Guardian*; p13 The Random House Group for an extract from *The Boys Are Back in Town* by Simon Carr, published by Hutchinson; p16 Atlantic Syndication for 'Cigarettes increase threat by 70%' from the *Daily Mail*, 4th October 2002; p18 News International Syndication for 'Go-Ahead for Wembley No. 2' by Diana Blamires, from the *Sun*, 27th September 2002 © NI Syndication Limited, London, 2002; p20 South Lakes Wild Animal Park for the use of extracts from their poster; p22 The *Independent* for 'Weather Map and chart' from the *Independent*, 25th September 2002; p26 Virgin Interactive, London for the use of Barbarian advert; p27 *Sugar* magazine for 'Facts' from *Sugar*, No 39, June 1998; p29 Everychild for the use of an appeal; P34 Barnardos for 'Abuse through prostitution steals children's lives'; p37 Telegraph Group Limited for the front page of the *Daily Telegraph*, Monday 23rd September, 2002 © Telegraph Group Limited, 2002; p38 The *Guardian* for 'Sailor survives after 4 months adrift' by Duncan Campbell, the *Guardian*, 26th September 2002 © The *Guardian*, 2002; p41 London Fire Brigade Firefighter Recruitment, for the use of their advert; p43 Hodder & Stoughton Limited for an extract from *Ancient Mysteries* by Rupert Matthews; Creative Publishing International Ltd for an extract from *Spine Tingling Tales*, published by Two-Can Publishing; p44 Hambleton Leisure Centre for extracts from their brochure; p46 Atlantic Syndication for 'Children denied a sporting chance' from the *Daily Mail*, Comment, 21st February 2002; p49 HMSO for Mind, Body & Soul extract © Crown Copyright 2003; p50 EMAP for a letter and reply from *Bliss* magazine, October 2001; *Health and Fitness* magazine for question and answer; *Men's Health* magazine for 'Eat fat stay slim'; p54 Oxford University Press, India for 'Night of the Scorpion' by Nissim Ezekiel, from *Poverty Poems*; p57 Tom Leonard for an extract from 'Unrelated Incidents' by Tom Leonard © Tom Leonard; p59 Dr Niyi Osundare for 'Not my Business' by Niyi Osundare from *Songs of the Seasons,* Heinemann Nigeria 1990 © Niyi Osundare; p64 Oxford University Press, UK for 'Limbo' by Kamau Braithwaite, from *The Arrivants: A New World Trilogy,* OUP 1973; p69 Curtis Brown Limited, London for 'Island Man' by Grace Nichols, from *The Fat Black Woman's Poems* © Grace Nichols 1984; p78 HMSO for 'Don't Lose Your Vote' © Crown Copyright; p79 Health Education Authority for two drugs posters; p84 Club 18-30 for extracts from their Summer 2003 brochure; pp93, 94 Shelter for the use of various extracts; p96 RSPCA for the use of their logo; Oxfam Publishing, 274 Banbury Road, Oxford OX44 7QY, for the use of their logo; Barnardos for the use of their logo; p99 EMAP for 'Your life sorted' from *Bliss* magazine, October 2001; p100 *Men's Health* magazine for 'Fighting Fit', *Men's Health*, July 2002; p102 Wexas Traveller for an extract from 'Staying alive: avoidable hassles' by Tony Bush and Ian Wilson, from *The Traveller's Handbook*, published by Wexas; p105 Harcourt Education for an extract from *World Focus: Jamaica* by John Baraclough; p106 Rough Guides Limited for an extract from 'Between Two Cultures' by Smita Patel, from *More Women Travel: A Rough Guide Special*; p117 The Random House Group Limited for an extract from *An Evil Cradling* by Brian Keenan, published by Hutchinson; p119 David Higham Associates Limited for an extract from *Going Solo* by Roald Dahl, published by Jonathan Cape & Penguin Books Limited; p121 Sheil Land Associates Limited for an extract from 'Mr Proudham and Mr Sleight' from *A Bit of Singing and Dancing* by Susan Hill, published by Hamish Hamilton © Susan Hill 1972; p125 WWF UK for 'Who cares what goes down the drain?'; p126 Aladdin Books Limited for an extract from *Pollution and Wildlife* (Survival Series); p138 Virgin Holidays, for the use of text and photographs about New York from their brochure.